THE DOVE CONNECTION

The Rest of Reagan

by
Edward E. Noble

HUNTINGTON HOUSE PUBLISHERS

Huntington House Publishers
P.O. Box 53788
Lafayette, Louisiana 70505

PRINTED IN THE UNITED STATES OF AMERICA

Library of Congress Card Catalog Number 97-77559
ISBN 1-56384-178-9

In Memory of Gary Allen

"... Between the mega-capitalists who lusted for control of world markets, and idealistic dreamers who expected somehow to solve the thorny problems that have always plagued mankind, there developed a symbiotic relationship. The result was a cooperative push toward world government. Both helped promote a New World Order under central political control, each for their own reasons.

"... Since [the proponents of world government] realize that their dream of a New World Order must be built on a religious foundation, they seek to replace traditional religions, Christianity in particular, with the religion of Humanism."*

* Gary Allen, *Say "No!" to the New World Order* (Seal Beach, CA: Concord Press, 1987), 23, 188.

Contents

Preface

This book can be thought of as a sequel to Gary Allen's *Say "No!" to the New World Order*. It identifies America's enemies, the enemies of freedom, most of whom are either Communists or those who aid and abet them—their only difference being a "formal" one, said Joseph Stalin, since "both serve the same common purpose." Who are these "non-Communists?"

Allen calls them the "mega-capitalists," who want to control the world's economy, and the "idealistic dreamers" (including doves), who want to solve mankind's problems. Thus a "symbiotic relationship" developed between them, resulting in "a cooperative push toward world government."

This "push toward world government" is what the Club of Rome (*Goals for Mankind*) calls "the world solidarity revolution," the goal of which is "a qualitatively new world order." While both capitalists and dreamers claim to want world peace, what the capitalists really want is an "all-powerful world socialist super-state" (with its new order), which, unknown to most dreamers, is also what the Communists want. What about world peace? Well, this comes with the superstate, according to former *Pravda* editor V.G. Afanasiev: "[The] Struggle for communism . . . is intrinsically bound up with the struggle for peace in the world." That is, "communism and world peace are inseparable."

This "qualitatively new world order" then would not be new at all, being the same oligarchical, collectivistic, monopolistic system known to man since the beginning of civilization—except for one thing: it would encircle the earth, leaving no room for rival systems, or for refuge. Actually, it would be nothing more than the Soviets' historic goal, worldwide Communism—though called world peace.

Since this book is also about Ronald Reagan (one of the dreamers), it provides a new perspective from which his presidency (if it was his) can be better understood.

Finally, the Soviet Union's new name, Russia, is not recognized since it has false connotations, one being that communism is dead.

ONE

Rocky-Bye-Baby

The belief that Ronald Reagan was a conservative president may be the most significant political delusion of this century—one having ominous consequences. Yet, millions of Americans, both liberals and conservatives, continue to cling to this belief, ignoring everything that invalidates it—while also meeting any attempt to alter it with incredulity.

This delusion can be somewhat understood by recalling the frustration and humiliation felt while waiting for the hostages in Iran to be released during President Carter's last years in office. Even America itself, being leaderless and in a socio-political vacuum, was a hostage, held for the fulfillment of Carter's idealistic and unconstitutional objectives. James Earl Carter, Jr., the "insufferable ass," as political essayist R. Emmett Tyrrell, Jr., calls him, was unacceptable to anyone with a sound, orderly mind. Tyrrell writes:

> During his whole bizarre regime, as the dollar sank and the Russians marched, there emanated from him the sense that nothing really mattered. Nothing beyond himself was real. There was no Iran, no Southeast Asia, no Russian military buildup. At the fag end of his four-year farce, in the hospital at Wiesbaden just before he met the hostages held for 444 days in our Teheran embassy, he was actually incredulous when informed that their Iranian captors had badly abused them.[1]

In contrast to his media-created "wonderboy" image, Carter was seen by many of us as an anathema to be painfully tolerated for four outrageous years, having been obscenely dumped upon us by the omnipresent "liberal" Eastern Establishment, largely represented by the David Rockefeller-dominated Council on Foreign Relations (CFR) and its international offshoot, the Trilateral Commission (TC).[2] This is confirmed by former Senator Barry M. Goldwater (R-AZ):

> Gerald Rafshoon, who served the Carter campaign as media expert, has said, "One of the most fortunate accidents in the early campaign and critical to his building support where it counted was Jimmy Carter's membership in the Trilateral Commission." It was no accident. Brzezinski [CFR/TC] and Rockefeller invited Carter to be a member of the Trilateral Commission in 1973. They immediately commenced grooming him for the presidency.[3]

By 1980 America had lost its national identity and millions of Americans were beginning to lose hope. They therefore wanted, or needed, to believe that Reagan really could and would "make America great again," as he had promised. His public image, unlike Carter's, was that of a man who was wise, realistic, confident, sincere, moral, compassionate, unpretentious, charming, easily forgivable, patriotic, God-fearing, and eternally young. This dream-like image remained intact during both of his terms. It was the payoff image, one that Reagan and much of the public symbiotically strived to preserve.

Thus, there were two Reagans: the creamy-dreamy one and the one Rockefeller and his operatives knew. Their private profiles revealed certain imperfections in him, which couldn't be found in the Reagan delusion. They knew, for instance, that he was not a man of strong character, being easy to co-opt, and easy to dupe, especially since he equated their world government (and new world order) with the kingdom of God, or something like it.

After being unable to sell insider George Bush (CFR/TC) in the 1980 Republican primaries, they then switched to Reagan, since Carter's re-election was unlikely. Therefore, long before November 1980, Reagan found himself and his administration-to-be being warmed and turned in the same old Rocky-Bye-Baby incubator that had produced the "insufferable one." While the Reagan egg was that of a Hollywood papier-mâché eagle, most of the others were those of buzzards, doves, and cuckoos.

In February, on the night of Reagan's New Hampshire victory, chief egg candler William J. Casey (CFR), a former chairman of the Export-Import Bank, became Reagan's campaign manager. This opened the door for others in the Rockefeller camp, such as Casey's "liberal" friend Donald T. Regan (CFR) who had been supporting Carter. In July, following the GOP convention, the Rocky-Bye-Baby Incubator Company's grade A jumbos began to hatch, some prematurely. Soon after breaking through their shells, Casper Weinberger (CFR/TC) and George Shultz (CFR) were admitted to the papier-mâché eagle's inner flock of advisors.

Meanwhile, heard pecking from within were Alexander Haig (CFR/TC), Malcolm Baldrige (CFR), James Baker (Bush's campaign manager), William Brock (CFR/TC), and Anne Armstrong (CFR). Shortly after the election, Regan was chosen for Treasury, an appointment that Conservative Caucus leader Howard Phillips called "a disgrace and insult to every person in America who worked for . . . Reagan's election."[4] Around the same time, *Human Events*, a Republican weekly, asked: "Why do the people surrounding the President-elect keep putting into the most important personnel slots those with distinctly non-conservative backgrounds? Simply put, why aren't the key selectors of personnel well-known conservatives?"[5] Why? Because, as *Human Events* must know, they work for the Rocky-Bye-Baby Incubator Co. (e.g., John J. McCloy CFR). Still, the most perfidious selection was the one that Reagan himself made at the convention. Though he had promised to choose a conservative running mate, he picked a "distinctly non conservative" one instead, George Bush. This, of course, means that he broke two promises since Bush was a Trilateralist. That is, when questioned during the Florida primary in March about using Trilateralists, Reagan replied:

> Now I don't believe that the Trilateral Commission is a conspiratorial group, but I do think its interests are devoted to international banking, multinational corporations, and so forth. I don't think that any administration of the U.S. government should have the top 19 positions filled by people from any one group or organization representing one viewpoint. No, I would go in a different direction.[6]

But he didn't—nor did he intend to. Along with Bush, about a dozen more Trilateralists also got jobs. As to Reagan's belief that the Commission is not conspiratorial, it is contrary to Goldwater's: "[The] Commission represents a skillful, coordinated effort to seize control and consolidate the four centers of power—political, monetary, intellectual, and ecclesiastical."[7] (This may be Reagan's "so forth.") Also, in contrast to Reagan's views, Goldwater states:

> What the trilateralists truly intend is the creation of a worldwide economic power superior to the political governments of the nation-states involved. They believe the abundant materialism they propose to create will overwhelm existing differences. As managers and creators of the system [a world government] they will rule the future.[8]

So Bush still ended up in the White House. Even his campaign manager, Baker, got in, having been made White House Chief of Staff. He was also in charge of Rocky-Bye-Baby's Office of Presidential Personnel, which controlled the political appointments. Some of his helpers were: Margaret Tutwiler, E. Pendleton James, Katherine J. Camalier, John S. Herrington, and Robert Tuttle. (Tuttle was the son of Reagan's close friend, Holmes Tuttle, a wealthy used car dealer. Robert's wife "was made undersecretary of commerce for travel and tourism."[9]) For non-insiders, the process dragged, starting with Tutwiler and ending with Tuttle. By the time they got to Tuttle, they were forgotten, having been reduced to mere names on 3x5 cards. Some were even told that their resumes were lost.

Thus the "Reagan Administration," largely composed of Bushites, became what would have been the Bush Administration. It was also, in this sense, the first two terms of Bush's three terms.[10] (This the Reaganuts still are unable to grasp.) The appointment process then was a waste of time, especially since there were only about three hundred sub-cabinet openings. Besides, most of these were reserved for Rocky-Bye's medium grade A's, while the lesser jobs went to the hatchees that peeped the loudest. Two years later, watchdog Paul Weyrich (Committee For The Survival Of A Free Congress) recalled how James "systematically froze out movement conservatives and encouraged the selection of warmed-over Trilateralist and C.F.R. types for posts throughout the government. Dozens of Reaganites who had labored for years in the political vineyards found themselves denied key support positions."[11]

Weyrich is highly respected among conservatives, and his opinion is seldom questioned. He also has a reputation for being objective. Above all, he is meticulous and principled. As described by a female PAC applicant in 1980, "My first impression as I entered Weyrich's office was that it was unpretentious. The walls were lined with books, most of them well-worn, and there were stacks and stacks of paper on the desks and tables. Still, the atmosphere was orderly, with absolutely no sense of confusion. Weyrich was courteous and, in spite of his dark suit and spanking white shirt, looked youthful. He said little and spoke softly; and as I spoke, he listened intently."[12]

However, Weyrich is not infallible. His pre-election analysis of Reagan, for instance, was largely subjective, being based on interviews, including some with Reagan. Still, because of the Reagan delusion, it was no worse than the other analyses, except for Gary Allen's. Though even Allen, a well-known political analyst, wasn't infallible. Like most of the other analysts, he too was baffled by Reagan, never quite sure who he really was. But, at least he admits it: "[In spite of] Reagan's many years in the political limelight . . . there is much we still do not know about him. Where does the actor stop and the real Reagan begin?"[13] Yet, he and Weyrich did agree on certain points:

> What then will a Reagan victory in November mean? Probably not nearly as much as most people believe. [Reagan] is not the Heaven-sent leader on a white horse who will slay the dragon of Big Government. . . . As Paul Weyrich observes, he is just not that kind of man. Despite his speeches, Reagan does not like controversy. He is not a gut fighter. He will not, for example, kill the Department of Energy, nor any other major bureau. . . .[14]

Weyrich's analysis was actually somewhat flattering. He described Reagan as "a sincere man with gut conservative instincts." He also called him "a man loyal to principle and . . . friends." However, he added: "but not ultimately loyal." By this, he meant: "[If] the opposition causes enough trouble, he will be willing to find a graceful way out of sticking to either principle or to friends." He didn't explain how one can be both loyal and not loyal. Similarly, he said that "Reagan is capable . . . of appointing some of the best men . . . in this country." Then, in the same breath: "But he is equally capable of appointing men who will make Conservatives gag." Weyrich didn't attribute this to immorality, but rather to imprudence.

Allen wasn't unkind to Reagan either. He was simply critical of him and, of course, suspicious. But, unlike Weyrich, he often asked questions like, "Is Reagan courting the Eastern 'Liberal' Establishment or is [it] attempting to co-opt him?" Even up to his death in November 1986, he was still unsure of Reagan, wondering just how much he really knew. In his last book, *Say "NO!" to the New World Order,* he asked: "How much does [Reagan] really know about how the Establishment . . . manipulate[s] U.S. foreign and domestic policies from behind the scenes?"[15]

Essentially, as Allen knew, nothing was much different than it would have been if Bush had been elected (or Carter reelected), except for an administration with a new name, different presidential style, and fresh hatchees from Rocky-Bye. The same Socialist, international agenda (leading to a new world order) was being pursued; and after the Hollywood "eagle" was gone, America (what was left of it) would still be waiting for someone to make it "great again." Allen had even predicted these things:

> It is only logical that the Insiders will try to apply the coup de grace against America through a Republican President simply because most people cannot believe that a Republican could be "soft on Communism" or would jeopardize our liberty or sovereignty. The watchdogs tend to go to sleep with a Republican in office.[16]

Weyrich's basic problem then is that he doesn't see things as Allen sees them. To Weyrich, there is no conspiracy.[17] There are simply Democrats who are liberals and Republicans who are either conservatives or moderates (i.e., pragmatists). And it's these moderates who somehow get the key appointments. That there's a correlation between getting them and belonging to Rocky-

Bye doesn't occur to him. Even eight years later, he still couldn't explain how these insiders got into Reagan's inner circle or why Reagan would want them. In Weyrich's way of thinking, things just sort of happen this way. However, he did admit that when "the Reagan administration has come to a close it will be evident to the merest political novice that little in the way of permanent change has been accomplished." Instead, he wrote,

> [with the exception of federal judge appointments] there is almost nothing this President has done which could not be wiped away by a single Democratic President working with solid liberal majorities in both houses of Congress. The Republican Party, the business PACs, and the conservative movement spent somewhere in the neighborhood of $1.5 billion over a decade to put Ronald Reagan in office, give him a Republican Senate, and then re-elect him to another term. It may soon be evident that we have little or nothing to show for it.[18]

Weyrich doesn't blame Rocky-Bye-Baby for this, or for anything else. He doesn't even consider its presence. Instead, he criticizes conservatives for having "so long resisted learning the art of governing—resisted using the power of government to accomplish our objectives." He ignores the fact that "the power of government" has been inaccessible, being in the hands of Rocky-Bye. That is, there exists a shadow government whereby only Rocky-Bye's agenda can be carried out. Weyrich also criticizes "those conservatives who simply hate government." He says: "Hatred of government has kept many of our conservative friends from even thinking about the process of governing. For those who believe in the Judeo-Christian ethic, hatred of government as an institution is not an option, and that's why I agree with George Will that those who hate government come close to hating their country."[19]

What is Weyrich really saying? Does he actually believe that true conservatives could hate "government as an institution"? As anarchists do? And what does he mean by "hatred"? Is he referring to critics of our unconstitutional government? Equating their righteous indignation with hatred? Even though it's out of love for their country?

But even when hatred of one's government (e.g., a Communist one) does exist, what does that have to do with hating one's country? A country is not a government. It *has* a government, while being a land inhabited by a certain people who have their own traditions. It may also have a constitution, their country's fundamental laws and principles, which their representatives, et al., being under oath, are expected to obey.

But what if they don't obey? Well, then the government becomes unconstitutional and oppressive, no longer deserving of the people's confidence and respect, though they still love their country, including its constitution, hating only the evil that has befallen it.

So why Weyrich agrees with George Will is somewhat unclear. While for Will (CFR/TC), "a frequent social guest of the Reagans,"[20] to say what he said is to be expected. Since his Rocky-Bye buddies run the government—which, unconstitutionally, now has four unchecked branches working together in sync, as it transforms itself (largely through its fourth branch, the regulatory agencies) into a totalitarian, Orwellian-like police state, already having the machinery in place for a takeover, including its many secretive, despotic Orders and Directives, 300 of which were "issued by Reagan."[21] As for Will, author/lecturer John F. McManus says that he "offers a stunning array of attitudes that will alternately delight and infuriate all but the schizophrenic. Yet he wants to be known as a conservative, which he is not. Instead, he is what he labels himself: a champion of 'strong government conservatism,' as tidy a contradiction as 'dry water.' " McManus adds: "Calling himself a

'Tory' who would have 'moved to Canada if I lived in Boston in 1772,' Will explains that the 'strong government conservatism' he favors is 'one that accepts the welfare state.' That puts him philosophically in tune with Ted Kennedy, Walter Mondale, and the Americans for Democratic Action."[22]

Reagan and his wife, Nancy, being "in awe of the eastern establishment," desired "to court social acceptability." That is, they "longed to be part of the ruling class exemplified by such mandarins as Katharine Graham [CFR/TC], publisher of the *Washington Post,* and New York philanthropist Brooke Astor." Also, according to the Reagans' aide Michael Deaver, Reagan "feels he not only wants to know [the power elites], but that he needs them."[23] Thus, Will, who became Reagan's "unofficial social director," spent much "energy introducing the [Reagans] to the people . . . he considered crucial to their social success" such as insiders Lane Kirkland (CFR/TC), Meg Greenfield (CFR), Robert Strauss (CFR/TC), and Douglas Dillon (CFR).[24]

The Reagans then were intimately involved with the insiders. This, logically, means that they were also influenced by them. Will, for instance, was a "dominant influence on [Nancy]," even being "her intellectual superior—aloof, articulate, and formidable."[25] Still, they were very close, often having lunch together. On one occasion, they went to Shepherdstown, West Virginia, about 60 miles away.[26] She even gave him an 8x10 photo of herself "in a glittery gown," which he "displays . . . in his office." On it, she wrote: "And the little girl grew up and began going out to lunch with a well-known columnist in Washington. Rest is history. LOVE."[27]

Thus, in a sense, the Reagans themselves became insiders—and willingly. This is why they were surrounded by them throughout Reagan's two terms. While Nancy had much to do with this, Reagan apparently did not dissuade or deter her. Weyrich, of course, blamed it all on "Deaver and the First Lady" since he saw Reagan as "the first conservative President in fifty years." Yet, if Reagan were truly conservative, he wouldn't have had an ultra-liberal aide like Deaver, nor allowed him to choose guests for the dinners and parties in the White House family quarters. Most of these guests were "liberal members of the [Republican] party, such as David Rockefeller and Henry Kissinger." Such "liberal Democrats as Katharine Graham" were also invited.[28] Reagan was totally at ease with them and enjoyed their company. They were friends. He felt and, in some ways, even thought the way they did. This fraternization continued even after leaving office. For instance, as *USA Weekend* reported (23-25 June 1989), only a few people "have entered the Reagans' inner sanctum [668 (formerly 666) St. Cloud Road, Bel-Air] so far," such as Henry Kissinger (CFR/TC), Colin Powell (CFR), Dick Thornburgh (CFR), and his wife, Ginny.[29]

One can only imagine what the topics of conversation were during Kissinger's visit. Perhaps Kissinger's January 1989 trip to Moscow was mentioned. He, along with David Rockefeller, had attended the Trilateral Commission meeting there. Later, Kissinger flew to Washington for a meeting with President Bush during his "first working Saturday afternoon."[30] Though this meeting was probably related to the Trilateralists' meeting, it must have also concerned Kissinger's meeting with Gorbachev while in Moscow. As the Soviet news agency Tass reported, Kissinger and Gorbachev met to discuss ideas "set forth by Kissinger on behalf of U.S. President-elect George Bush."[31]

Another topic may have been the new commission "set up by the U.S. Government to 'study military strategies for the next century.' "[32] Three of its members were John Vessey (CFR), Zbigniew Brzezinski (CFR/TC), and, of course, Kissinger. How they knew who our enemies would be, in order to determine such strategies, was unclear. But, now we know. According to *The Fact Finder* (1 September 1994), "From two sources recently we've heard that . . . Clinton issued PDD-25 on May 5, placing United States Military Forces under United Nations command. This directive was pushed through after General Colin Powell resigned."[33]

Kissinger may have also mentioned the mysterious construction taking place in Canberra, Australia, under Harvey Rockefeller's supervision. This project, which included the building of twenty-two large mansions, was financed by the Rockefeller Foundation. Since Canberra is the site of highly advanced computer operations, and "has worldwide connections," this project was possibly related to changes in the global power structure.[34]

Kissinger's plan to build a $50 million railroad from Communist Zimbabwe to Communist Mozambique also would have interested Reagan, since he had approved of it. Apparently, it was his way of "making America great again." In the 3 August 1988 *Federal Register*, he stated: "I hereby certify that it is in the national interest of the United States to make available for activities in Mozambique funds from the $50,000,000 appropriated to assist sector projects supported by the Southern African Development Coordination Conference (SADCC) to enhance the economic development of [SADCC's] member states. . . ."[35] He was actually saying that financing a Communist railroad (that bypassed South Africa's seaports) would be to our advantage.

The topics available were inexhaustible, considering Kissinger's endless intrusion in our nation's affairs, foreign and domestic. As one observer put it, "This man is really running our country, and you better believe it!" Kissinger's nest is well-feathered, which is not unrelated to his intimate association with Rocky-Bye-Baby. His firm, Kissinger Associates, Inc., earns at least $62 million annually, being retained by about 250 corporations for $250 thousand each (e.g., American Express, American International, Rockefeller's Chase Manhattan Bank, Continental Grain, Fiat, Hunt Oil, H. J. Heinz, ITT, Midland Bank of England). Kissinger is also "a trustee of the Rockefeller Fund, a member of the international advisory board of the Chase Manhattan Bank, a board member of American Express, Continental Grain, R. H. Macy, and Union Pacific."[36]

Retired Army Lt. General Colin Powell, one of the other guests, was Reagan's national security assistant. He was selected for permanent membership in the Council on Foreign Relations during the 1985-1986 fiscal year. The chairman of the council's membership committee then was retired Air Force Lt. General Brent Scowcroft (CFR/TC),[37] Bush's national security advisor. Before this, Scowcroft was vice-chairman of Kissinger Associates, Inc., while also running Kissinger's Washington office.[38] His positions with the Kissinger firm and Bush administration were probably related. In 1976, Allen wrote:

> Increasing concern over the amount of power Kissinger possessed, however, caused the Secretary of State to doff his other hat, that as director of the National Security Council, last year. But the fact that the NSC directorship passed to a long-time Kissinger protege, Lt. General Brent Scowcroft, makes the gesture virtually meaningless. Senator Henry M. Jackson . . . noted that "Despite the appearances, Kissinger will retain full control of the National Security Council."[39]

Both Kissinger and Scowcroft presided over Council on Foreign Relations' meetings during the 1985-1986 fiscal year, when Powell became a Council member. Kissinger chaired the 22 October 1985, "Roundtable Luncheon" whereat Mohammed Zia-ul-Haq (President of Pakistan) spoke on "Regional Balance in South Asia."[40] Zia, friend of the anti-Soviet Afghan resistance movements, died on 17 August 1988 in an aircraft explosion due to Soviet sabotage. Also killed was Arnold Raphel, U.S. ambassador to Pakistan. State Secretary Shultz, backed by Reagan, "vetoed the sending of trained FBI investigators" to the crash site, probably to keep the Soviets from being incriminated.[41]

Scowcroft headed the 3 October 1985 "Roundtable" featuring Trilateralist Lord Carrington (Chairman, North Atlantic Council; Secretary-General, NATO), whose topic was "NATO: The Year Ahead."[42] Carrington, "a very wealthy banker," (Hambros Bank) and Bilderberger par excellence,[43] also ran the 21 November 1985 "General Meeting" at which Zbigniew Brzezinski lectured on "The Summit: An Assessment."[44]

Brzezinski is Kissinger's ideological clone. Both were national security advisors (and security risks). They are also zealous proponents of a new world order. "Like Kissinger," notes columnist Paul Scott, "Brzezinski believes that 'a new pattern of international politics is emerging' which will 'curb national sovereignty' and lead toward the development of a 'new international order.' "[45] They are also select agents of the Rockefeller Dynasty. While Brzezinski is to David Rockefeller what Kissinger was to Nelson, they all shared the same Orwellian dream: a totalitarian world government—with themselves in charge. Nelson even admitted in 1968 that, if he were president, "he would work toward international creation of 'a new world order' based on East-West cooperation instead of conflict."[46] Similarly, in 1989, David said, "I believe the climate is right and the stage set for our nations to come together in a Congress of the New World."[47]

Brzezinski, like Kissinger, is obsessed with the idea of power, and "is shown by his admissions to be a conspirator laboring to abolish our country and replace it with a dictatorship."[48] To Brzezinski, everything, animate and inanimate, should be state-controlled, even the atmosphere. Having admitted that he accepts "the idea of a vast expansion in social regulation," he states: "It may take such forms as legislation for the number of children, perhaps even legislation determining the sex of children once we have a choice, the regulation of weather, the regulation of leisure, and so forth,"[49] which is precisely how Lenin, Stalin, and der Fuehrer felt.

In his book, *Between Two Ages,* Brzezinski implies that the "gradual shaping of a community of the developed nations" should be accompanied by the: (1) blurring of "traditional distinctions between governmental and nongovernmental social processes"; (2) promotion through "educational reforms" of "rational humanist values"; (3) promotion of "global consciousness"; (4) dissemination of "scientific and technological knowledge" as "a more functional approach to man's problems, emphasizing ecology rather than ideology" (with the exception of humanism, of course). According to Brzezinski, a global consciousness, with scientific knowledge, will "help to encourage the spread of a more personalized rational humanist outlook that would gradually replace the institutionalized religious, ideological, and intensely national perspectives that have dominated modern history."[50]

Unlike most Polish-Americans, Brzezinski (who was naturalized in 1958[51]) is not patriotic. In fact, he doesn't even like America, particularly its Constitution. He sees it as an obstacle to the many changes he wants to make in "the nation's formal institutional framework." These changes, as he implies, would make America more like Europe: ". . . [The] increasingly international experience of the American intellectual and business elite [which he identifies with] has [led them] to consider contemporary problems within a larger framework, [hence learning from] the political evolution and the social innovation of other advanced countries. . . ." For instance, "it is now more candidly admitted that America has much to learn from Western Europe in metropolitan planning, in local urban planning, in regionalization, in the development of new towns, and in social and legal innovation."[52]

He is also concerned about the "cultural aspects of American society," such as education's "shaping of national values." He feels that education should promote his own worldview, which he calls "a rationalist humane outlook." "This rational humanism," he says, "is expressed . . . in an emerging international consciousness that [makes one] go beyond purely nationalistic concerns." Moreover, it views "international problems as human issues and not as political confrontations between good and evil." While seeking a "more philosophical and religiously ecumenical [definition] of human nature," it recognizes the need for "cultural and economic global diversity."[53]

Thus, Brzezinski was hoping that the two-hundredth anniversary of either the Declaration of Independence or the U.S. Constitution would "justify the call for a national constitutional convention to re-examine [both] the nation's formal institutional framework" and its "cultural aspects." There would be a redefining of the "meaning of modern democracy" and the setting of "ambitious and concrete social goals." There would also be a discussion of the: (1) "relevance of existing arrangements"; (2) "workings of the representative process"; (3) "desirability of imitating the various European regionalization reforms"; (4) "streamlining [of] the administrative structure." However, says Brzezinski, "[realism] forces us to recognize that the necessary political innovation will not come from direct constitutional reform, desirable as that would be. The needed change is more likely to develop incrementally and less overtly [i.e., more covertly]."[54]

Dick Thornburgh, who also "entered the Reagans' inner sanctum," has much in common with Brzezinski. He doesn't like our Constitution either and wants America to be more like Europe. This is why he joined the Committee on the Constitutional System (CCS), "an elite organization devoted to transforming [our] republican form of government into a European-style parliamentary democracy."[55] But, why then did Reagan invite him into his "inner sanctum"? After all, didn't Reagan, as president, swear that he would "to the best of [his] ability, preserve, protect and defend the Constitution of the United States"? Well, yes, but he also tried, "to the best of [his] ability," to change it. In addition to recommending a balanced-budget amendment to the Constitution,[56] he also tried to prevent Alabama from repealing "a 1976 Act that petitioned Congress to convene a Constitutional Convention." That is, after the Alabama legislature passed House Joint Resolution 26 on 28 April 1988, which repealed the act, Reagan "phoned Alabama Governor Guy Hunt and asked him to 'veto' the bill," even though, according to Alabama's attorney general: "From a review of the [U.S. Constitution] and Alabama law, the Governor appears to have no legal role."[57]

What does a balanced-budget amendment have to do with changing the Constitution? Well, actually nothing. But pretending to want one does. Take Reagan for example. Why would he want such an amendment, considering that he himself never tried to balance the budget? Yet, if he didn't really want one, what did he want? Here's how a 1988 American Freedom Movement (AFM) newsletter explained it: "One of the [amendment's] biggest backers . . . is our 'conservative' President Reagan who, incidentally, hasn't proposed a balanced budget in any of [his] eight years . . . in office! An interesting sidelight to this is [Thornburgh's appointment] to replace Ed Meese as Attorney General. Thornburgh testified before [a New Jersey legislative committee] on 21 October 1986, in support of the Constitutional Convention! [He] said,

> "The executive and legislative branches [are] caught up in a system badly in need of structural adjustment. The balanced budget amendment is the key element in such an adjustment."

> Read that statement again. What Thornburgh said is that [the amendment is] the "key element" [in opening up the] Constitution . . . to "structural

adjustment." There it is. These New World Order people want to change our system [and] are using the "balanced budget" issue [to do it].[58]

But wait! Certainly the head of the Department of Justice, who is America's chief legal representative and advisor, and who runs everything from the FBI to Interpol-Washington, wouldn't want to dump our system of government and Constitution, "the supreme Law of the Land"! After all, didn't Thornburgh, like the other federal officials, solemnly swear to defend the Constitution and, in his case, enforce it? And what about Reagan and Bush? Didn't they also swear to "preserve, protect, and defend the Constitution of the United States"? Yes, they did. Well, then wouldn't this mean that Thornburgh's appointment somehow helped them to do it? Well, not exactly. You see, Thornburgh's background includes being director of the Urban League, the Neighborhood Legal Services, and the Greater Pittsburgh branch of the ACLU. He was also chairman of the Western Pennsylvanians for Rockefeller (Nelson for President) Committee. And there's something else. According to the AFM newsletter,

> [There] are two things which must be completed before our nation can be subverted: (1) remove the guns from the citizens and (2) consolidate the local police forces into a large federal police force. The first is obvious, and the second is becoming more obvious—the New World Order necessity for a KGB or Gestapo. Richard Thornburgh has worked tirelessly to achieve . . . these agenda items.[59]

Thornburgh then was helping Bush "to prepare for [in Bush's words] the new world that begins eleven short years from now." Bush even admitted that "[preparing for it is] what my agenda is all about."[60] This is what he meant in his inaugural address by "a new breeze is blowing." Actually, it was the same hot air Ron and

Gorby stirred up during their Washington-Moscow "love-ins." Bush's metaphor, therefore, was complementary to the "we-changed-a-world" imagery in Reagan's farewell address. Whereas Reagan said, "we have, over the past few years, forged a satisfying new closeness with the Soviet Union [since Gorby is different than his predecessors]," Bush claimed "a new breeze is blowing and a world refreshed by freedom seems reborn; for in man's heart, if not in fact, the day of the dictator is over." He added, effusively:

> The totalitarian era is passing, its old ideas blown away like leaves from an ancient, lifeless tree. A new breeze is blowing and a nation refreshed by freedom stands ready to push on. There's new ground to be broken [graves?] and new action to be taken [in Tiananmen Square, Ruby Ridge, and Waco?].[61]

Is Bush saying that communism is dead? That the Gulag has been dismantled? That Red China's slave labor camps are gone? That Cuba, N. Korea, and Vietnam are now nations "refreshed by freedom"? That the UN is defunct? That America's sovereignty is no longer threatened? That the Constitution and its first ten amendments are being observed? That states' rights and individual freedom have been restored? Where is this "new breeze" blowing?

Is Bush's "new world" the same as Brzezinski's "community of the developed nations"? Both concepts include the Soviet Union and other Communist states. Besides, Bush also refers to his idea as a "community of nations." Addressing graduates of the U.S. Coast Guard Academy on 24 May 1989, he cooed (after falsely claiming that, through the policy of "containment," the U.S. had been "checking" Soviet expansionism up until recent times):

> You are graduating into an exciting world where the opportunity for peace, world peace, lasting

peace, has never been better. Our goal—integrating the Soviet Union into the community of nations—is every bit as ambitious as containment was at its time, and it holds tremendous promise for international stability.[62]

Let's see now . . . "integrating the Soviet Union into the community of nations." This is "our goal," and it would lead to "world peace." But why would America want to be part of a "community" that included Communist nations, especially the most powerful one? Isn't communism "a political doctrine based on revolutionary Marxian socialism"?[63] But wait! Maybe it's the other way around. That the "community" is the "world of Communism," which wants to include us in it. At least maybe that's the way they see it. This would explain what *Pravda*'s former editor-in-chief, V. G. Afanasiev, meant when he said that "communism and world peace are inseparable."[64]

And didn't Gorbachev tell the Central Committee that they were "moving toward a new world, the world of Communism [and would] never turn off that road"?[65] Could it be that Gorbachev's "new world" is the same as Bush's "new world," which is "what [his] agenda [was] all about"? If it is, then the Soviets (and all other Communists) see Rocky-Bye's new world order as "the world of Communism." They would also see it as the "community" that Soviet spokesman A. Solodovnikov mentioned: "The concept of a future in which capitalism and communism will 'converge' on an 'equal footing' is utopian through and through. The time will come, of course, when there will be a world government, but it will be the government of a world Socialist (Communist) community."[66]

A convergence of capitalism and communism has long been Rocky-Bye's dream. This was even conceded in 1953 by the Ford Foundation's president, H. Rowan Gaither (CFR), when he said "every effort [was being made] to so alter life in the United States as to make possible a comfortable merger with the Soviet Union." But what he didn't say was that this merger would lead to Solodovnikov's "world government . . . of a world socialist (Communist) community."[67]

All of this, said Solodovnikov, was just a matter of time. He was right, it seems, for the merger has begun. This is what Senator Jesse Helms (R-NC) was telling his colleagues on 15 December 1987. But they weren't listening. They were thinking about the cushy jobs awaiting them in the many onion-like layers of global government. They would someday, hopefully, be nomenklaturists—our unelected rulers. Still, Helms explained how the Washington (INF) summit (8-10 December 1987) marked "the initiation of a new phase in Soviet-American relations" and was meant "to produce a convergence in the two systems." He said this "detente offensive [was] twofold":

> First, it is a means to promote a broad array of financial and commercial relations between American business and the Kremlin which will keep the Soviet empire afloat. . . .

> Second . . . [it] is a means to promote cultural change in the United States in order to so alter our traditional way of life that a convergence or merging of the American and Soviet systems can occur.[68]

This "detente offensive" was associated with Gorbachev's *glasnost* (i.e., propaganda, not openness) and *perestroika* (i.e., restructuring). However, to Gorbachev, such restructuring means revolution, not just in the Soviet Union but everywhere. For instance, he writes: "We know that we in this world are . . . now linked to the same destiny, that we live on the same planet. . . . For the whole world needs restructuring." But it must begin in our minds: "A new way of thinking must develop. . . . Revolutions always begin in the mind . . . in liberating the mind." What is this "new way of thinking"? Well, it isn't exactly thinking. It's being aware, or conscious of—uh, something . . . and in "a new way." Author Texe Marrs explains it:

> Enthusiastically endorsing the world peace movement, [Gorbachev says] that the issue of disarmament and world peace "can and must rally mankind, and facilitate the formation of a global consciousness."

> He further makes clear that his concept of global consciousness is the same as that of such fervent [New Agers] as Benjamin Creme, David Spangler, and Barbara Marx Hubbard.[69]

Thus, under New Ageism's influence, this "detente offensive" had another, less visible, dimension. However, within its secular context, it had evolved from the Geneva summit (19-21 November 1985), which led to the INF (intermediate-range nuclear forces) treaty. Reagan and Gorbachev, for instance, had agreed "to cut offensive nuclear arms by 50 percent in appropriate categories."[70] They also signed *The General Agreement between* [the U.S.-U.S.S.R.] *on Contacts, Exchanges and Co-operation in Scientific, Technical, Educational, Cultural and Other Fields.*[71]

These merger-oriented U.S.-U.S.S.R. agreements, which promoted the Soviet normative system, encouraged fraternization between scholars, teachers, and other professionals, in the usual academic, technical, and vocational fields. This included art exhibitions, ballet performances, concerts, film festivals, and sport events. Later, *Human Events* remarked:

> President Reagan didn't give away his Strategic Defense Initiative at the Geneva summit . . . but he did sign a series of cultural and exchange agreements that have made left-wingers and peaceniks in this country nearly euphoric.

> Writing in a recent issue of *Surviving Together,* a journal that promotes U.S.-Soviet contacts, Harriet

> Crosby [of the Institute for Soviet-American Rela-
> tions] said the Reagan-Gorbachev agreements will
> spark "the most far-reaching set of contacts in the
> history of U.S.-Soviet relations."
>
> "It is now possible," Crosby said, "that we will
> witness an easing of tensions, a normalization of
> relations, and a weaving together of the fabric of
> our two societies."[72]

Reagan's pre-summit briefing on 7 November 1985 was given by six specialists, four of whom were members of the Council on Foreign Relations: James H. Billington, Arnold L. Horelick, Richard E. Pipes, and William G. Hyland.[73] Hyland, who is also a Trilateralist, is a former editor of *Foreign Affairs*, the CFR's quarterly. He is also a senior fellow of the Carnegie Endowment for International Peace, which funds the Bilderberg conferences.[74]

After the summit, Rocky-Bye's U.S.-U.S.S.R. Trade and Economic Council met in Moscow. There was also a 1986 meeting between the Council on Foreign Relations and the Soviet Institute for the Study of the U.S.A. and Canada. About 40% of the Institute's staff were "working under the direct supervision of the KGB."[75] Other summit-related developments were: (1) The establishment of an exchange program for high-ranking American and Soviet military officers; (2) a meeting between the American Bar Association and the Association of Soviet Lawyers; (3) and an agreement between the National Academy of Sciences and the Soviet Academy of Sciences to conduct conferences, exchanges, and workshops on scientific issues.[76]

Though related, the Geneva and Washington summits had more to do with disarmament (e.g., INF Treaty) and State Department Publication 7277 (*Freedom From War*), concerning the "program for [achieving] general and complete disarmament in a peaceful world." This program's purpose is to disarm the nations, including the people, "to a point where [they would be unable] to challenge the progressively strengthened U.N. Peace Force."[77] This is the reason for today's gun control legislation, which Reagan supports.[78] It is also why state and local law enforcement agencies are insidiously being federalized.

However, this unchallengeable "peace" force would belong to Solodovnikov's world Communist "community." Naturally State's publication doesn't mention this. It simply predicts "a peaceful world." "World peace" though, says Afanasiev, is inseparable from communism. Just as Bush's "new world" (or "community of nations") is inseparable from Gorbachev's "world of Communism" wherein, proclaims Bush, there will be "peace, world peace, lasting peace."

Was Bush aware of all this when (at a 9 January 1991 press conference) he said the "new world order . . . is only going to be enhanced if this newly activated peacekeeping function [Desert Storm] of the United Nations proves to be effective"? Why, of course. He admits it. This is what "[his] agenda [was] all about." That is, he was preparing "for the new world." Now Clinton (CFR/TC) is doing it, as evident in his 27 September 1993 UN speech.

What about Reagan? Was he doing it too? Well, yes and no. It depends on which Reagan, the real one or the one who made America "great again." The latter, though delusional, is the one Rocky-Bye's propaganda mill continues to sustain. For example, *The World Almanac*, which claims to be a book of facts, says that central to his "foreign policy was the prevention of communist expansion," such as his "support of the Contras." Then, as proof of this, it quotes him: "At every point on the map that the Soviets have applied pressure, we've done all we can to apply pressure against them. . . . And now we are seeing a sight many believed they would never see in our lifetime: the receding of the tide of totalitarianism."[79]

Anyone who believes this would be a likely prospect for *that bridge*. None of these "facts" are facts, for they are totally incongruous with what actually happened. Take Nicaragua, for instance. The only pressure there was on the CIA/State-controlled Contras since they were not allowed to destabilize the Soviet-backed Sandinistas. That is, like Korea, the Bay of Pigs, and Vietnam, they were in a no-win situation, which in itself is pressure. Why weren't they allowed to win? Because the real Reagan's real objective was a "negotiated peace" (i.e., sellout). How do we know? Reagan said so:

> We do not seek the military overthrow of the Sandinista government. . . .
>
> Our policy is . . . to secure democracy [i.e., socialism] and lasting peace through national dialogue and regional negotiations.[80]

Why then did the Contras need assistance? After all, what was there to do? One thing. To act like Contras, since they were part of the Hegelian dialectic process: thesis vs. antithesis = synthesis. In other words, there had to be two opposing forces (i.e., Contras vs. Sandinistas) in order to effect Rocky-Bye's predetermined solution (i.e., a "negotiated peace," or takeover). Nuclear arms buildups/negotiations also work this way. By creating two opposing nuclear arsenals, a problem (i.e., threat to world peace) was fabricated to fit the ready-made solution (i.e., disarmament, followed by world government), in accordance with State's *Freedom From War*.

Thus, in no way were the Soviets pressured. It was just the opposite. All their needs were satisfied: money, food (e.g., wheat), technology, and especially time.[81] But wait! What about containment? Didn't Bush tell the 1989 Coast Guard Academy graduates that we had a containment policy which "we [now] have a precious opportunity to move beyond"?[82] Yes, he did, but it wasn't communism that was being contained, as he implied. It was anti-communism.

So, in this sense, there was containment, not only in Nicaragua but also in Afghanistan, Angola, Mozambique, South Africa, and anywhere else "on the map [where] the Soviets . . . applied pressure." In Nicaragua, for example, Reagan's role was merely to "stall for time," which would enable the Soviets/Sandinistas to consolidate their position. As one credible source observed,

> In 1980 the Insiders [i.e., Rocky-Bye-Baby] needed to give the Soviet Union time to pour in armaments, train a 60,000 man army, and build seaports and airfields. They needed to give the Sandinistas time to terrorize and subdue the people, institute a draft, suppress the Catholic church, fill the schools with propaganda, control all means of communication, and hold a fraudulent election to give themselves "legitimacy." [It is now] clear that [Reagan's] real purpose . . . through Congress was simply to provide this essential time.[83]

But what about all that money the Contras got? Why so much? Well, actually, compared to what the Soviets gave the Sandinistas, it was mere pocket-change. Whereas, during Reagan's two terms, the Contras got around $200 million, the Sandinistas received about $4 billion, a 1:20 ratio. The Contras would have had more if it hadn't been illegally diverted, which was also a problem in Afghanistan: "In 1987 allegations were made . . . that only $390 million of the $1.09 billion of aid approved by Congress between 1980 and 1986 to support the Mujahideen [i.e., Afghan freedom fighters] had actually reached them. [It was also] said that between 1980 and 1984 of the $342 million appropriated by Congress, only $36 million of military aid arrived in Afghanistan. . . ." One official remarked: "Maybe somebody wanted the money to go to the Nicaraguan Contras, but Contra leaders say even Ollie North's money didn't reach them. The question is, where is the money? Where did the $700 million go?"[84]

Aid to the Mujahideen was cut off even before the 14 April 1988 Afghan "peace" agreement in Geneva. They were also denied official recognition, and thus kept from participating in the negotiations. The Soviets' puppet government was recognized instead. Later, Reagan boasted about the settlement, while ignoring the Soviets' genocidal slaughter of over 1¼ million helpless human beings.

The freedom fighters in Angola (UNITA) and Mozambique (RENAMO) got the same treatment. While receiving a few handouts, their Communist-controlled governments were being financed by the U.S. Export-Import Bank, the World Bank (IRBD), and the International Monetary Fund (IMF). This was in addition to Soviet-bloc support. Reagan knew all this, since everyone else did or could have.

Meanwhile, Communist leaders were being invited to the White House, praised, and treated like heroes. Mozambique's Red dictator, Samora Machel, for instance, was favorably compared to—of all people—Abraham Lincoln. Moreover, during his September 1985 White House visit, he was offered military assistance even though he was already getting it from the Soviet Union, East Germany, Bulgaria, Zimbabwe, Cuba, North Korea, and North Vietnam. While a Vietnamese general ran his air force, the East Germans flew the planes, controlled the information services, and "established the state secret police, SNASP, which runs Mozambique's prisons and re-education camps, home to an estimated 300,000 captives." Censuring the Reagan-Machel meeting, Howard Phillips remarked:

> Machel has endorsed the Soviet occupation of Afghanistan, the Palestine Liberation Organization and the Sandinistas. There is no Soviet objective or policy worldwide from which Machel has disassociated himself. . . .

The Machel government is being effectively opposed by RENAMO, an indigenous anti-Communist resistance movement which supports religious
liberty, protection of private property, and racial
equality. For Ronald Reagan [who has rhetori-
cally backed anti-Communist freedom movements]
to support a Moscow-backed tyranny against a
native people's struggle for independence is the
ultimate hypocrisy.[85]

Reagan's hypocrisy did not begin or end with
Mozambique. It was evident throughout his presidency,
such as when he betrayed South Africa, an anti-Communist ally, which would not have been done were it not
anti-Communist. Though beleaguered from without by
Rocky-Bye and its pro-Communist affiliates (including
the political-Left church), it fell from within by way of
the South African Communist Party (SACP) and its proxy,
the African National Congress (ANC), et al.

Such hypocrisy was also evident during his early
betrayal of the anti-Communist Republic of China (Taiwan) when, on 17 August 1982, he issued a joint com-
munique with Communist China acknowledging it as
China's "sole legal government," and that "Taiwan is
part of [it]," which was soon followed by Export-Import
Bank loans and high-technology transfers.[86] All of this,
he said, would "strengthen the security of the United
States and promote *world peace* [emphasis mine]."[87] And
it would, per communism's inversion of terms, that
"world peace [and communism] are inseparable."[88]

Of course, to those who believe *The World Almanac*,
none of this is true. They read that Reagan took "a
strong anti-Communist stance,"[89] as in his "[support for]
El Salvador, the Nicaraguan contras, and other anti-
Communist governments and forces throughout the
world,"[90] which, besides being an overstatement, is an
inappreciable part of the story. As for El Salvador, the
Almanac doesn't tell them that Reagan helped José
Napoleon Duarte, a Socialist, "win his 1984 election

over the anti-Communist Roberto d'Aubuisson."[91] Naturally, this didn't keep Rocky-Bye's *New York Times* from claiming that the *Almanac* provides "accurate information on an endless array of subjects."[92]

Missing from this "endless array" is that Reagan made no attempt to bring our POW's and MIA's home from Southeast Asia. All evidence of them, including sightings, was rejected or ignored. Eventually, they were declared dead, whether they were or not, in order to appease their captors (now thought of as our "former" enemies).

Actually, in a sense, Reagan was bringing their captors home. That is, numerous high-ranking Soviet and Communist Chinese officers were being invited to tour, and inspect, various U.S. military installations, places where many of our POW's and MIA's had been. Some of these officers may have even seen them (or known of their whereabouts), especially since the Soviet Union signed a "friendship treaty" with Communist Vietnam on 3 November 1978.

This betrayal continued under Bush and Clinton, even though, as commanders-in-chief, they were in charge of our military, including captured and missing personnel. That is, without any sense of loyalty to them, they treasonably provided the enemy with "aid and comfort," especially through complicity in the detainment of our POW's.

Also in Rocky-Bye's dialectic memory hole are the 269 victims (including 61 Americans) of the Soviets' 1 September 1983 KAL 007 atrocity. Many of them were children, as at Waco. Still, like the POW's and MIA's, all of these people were declared dead, whether they were or not—and for the same reason, which is why Rocky-Bye's prostitute press still falsely claims that the Soviets "shot a South Korean airliner out of the sky . . . killing all 269 people aboard."[93]

But it was not "shot out of the sky" nor were all of the people killed. After its #4 engine was hit by a heat-seeking missile, it remained aloft for at least twelve minutes.[94] Although there is evidence that it landed on Sakhalin, a Soviet island in the Sea of Japan, one leading authority says it landed near Sakhalin in shallow water and "did not sink." He also claims "the passengers and crew were transported to a coast guard base," eventually "[disappearing] in the KGB hiding-places."[95]

Considering the innocence of these people, how can the attack on 007 be explained? What was its purpose? Well, according to the Soviets (and their State Department apologists), it was just a mistake (i.e., 007 was mistaken for a military plane and/or mistakenly believed to be on a spy mission). However, it was not a mistake. Otherwise, why the cover-up? Actually, the airliner probably had been targeted long before reaching the Sakhalin area. Why? Because the Soviets, et al., wanted one of its passengers, Congressman Larry McDonald (D-GA), dead. So their plan was simply to shoot the plane down, which would have been "cleaner." But they goofed.

McDonald, like Senator Jesse Helms, was one of Congress' most outspoken anti-Communists. He was also chairman of the anti-Communist John Birch Society (JBS), named after U.S. Army Captain John M. Birch, a World War II hero (Legion of Merit). Birch, who served in China with General Chennault's Flying Tigers, was executed by the Communist Chinese ten days after the war.

The Soviets therefore hated JBS as much as they did McDonald. This is why Khrushchev declared, during his 1959 visit, that all JBS members should be made to suffer "the torments of hell,"[96] which is how Communists feel about most people, including each other.

Like Helms, the politically-incorrect McDonald was also despised, and somewhat feared, by the political-Left, particularly Rocky-Bye, for not being—well, politically correct. Like the Soviets, they too were happy to get rid of McDonald, while expressing little, if any, sorrow over 007's innocent passengers. Such callousness is symptomatic of the revolutionary conscience, associated with the end-justifies-the-means ism. Thus, the Left and the Soviets had the same reasons for wanting McDonald out of the way. As a Christian and patriot, he was an obstacle to their revolutionary cause. They were particularly disturbed by his open opposition to communism, detente, and U.S.-U.S.S.R. trade. The KGB even kept a file on him, watching every move he made.[97] They undoubtedly also had one on Helms. But why then wasn't he on the flight too? He was, or sort of. As reported in Lawrence Patterson's newsletter, *A Monthly Lesson in Criminal Politics:*

> One quickly gains an understanding of what it means to be a patriot after hearing one of Sen. Helms' talks! . . . He spoke in detail about the Chilean situation and explained the incredible attacks on him by the globalist conspiracy utilizing the *NYT* [*New York Times*] and *Washington Post.*

> Sen. Helms was scheduled to be on [Korean Air Lines Flight 007] with Congressman Lawrence McDonald—and was only saved by a last minute re-routing. . . . Both McDonald and Helms were to attend a S. Korean-U.S. friendship celebration at the request of (now get this)—*Ronald Reagan!*[98]

Does this mean that Reagan was an accomplice in an assassination attempt on McDonald and Helms? No, it doesn't. But such complicity is not inconceivable. After all, he was an accomplice in the sellout of Nicaragua, Afghanistan, Angola, Mozambique, South Africa, and Taiwan. The lives of millions of freedom-loving people were negotiated away in these places. What's two more? And what about the POW's and MIA's? How much sympathy did he have for them and their loved ones?

Besides, we know now that Reagan was not a foe of communism. His relations with the various Communist regimes were actually cordial and non-threatening. That

is, he was non-confrontational, even accommodative—
the opposite of the Reagan delusion. For example, he
offered to share the SDI with the Soviets ("if and when
our research proves that [it] is practical"[99]) and, during
his return from Communist China on 1 May 1984, he
remarked,

> I found that *our* [emphasis mine] Chinese leaders
> I was talking with have no expansionist ideas at
> all. . . . So, as far as I'm concerned we can live at
> peace in the world together. If they prefer social-
> ism or communism and we prefer the democracy
> that we have—we may know that ours is best,
> but—we won't say that to them.[100]

His support for the pro-Communist United Nations, and faith in "its noble purposes," should also be
considered. In his 22 September 1986 UN address, he
praised its "devotion to the dream of world peace and
freedom, of human rights and democratic self-determination." Earlier, he had urged ratification of the treacherous UN-sponsored Genocide Convention (Treaty),
resulting in its approval on 19 February 1986. It didn't
bother him that the treaty allows government-perpe-
trated (and politically-motivated) genocide to go un-
punished. He must have known that it "was structured
from the beginning effectively to exempt Communist
governments, the only consistent perpetrators of genocide in the world. . . ."[101]

He must have known a lot of other things too, like
who was pulling the strings. And why and how they were
being pulled. Like other presidential puppets, he could
see the strings and feel their pull. But this suited him.
It was his means of animation, and he didn't have to
think. Besides, he had the leading role and liked the
script. He was also well-paid and had an eight-year
contract—oh, and that multimillion-dollar Bel-Air mansion awaiting him.[102]

While with Rocky-Bye's "New World Theatre of
Puppetry," Reagan's greatest performance was a two-act

show called "Amerika in the Making," for which he received a "Vladimir." Acts I and II took place in Washington (8-10 December 1987) and Moscow (29 May, 2 June 1988) respectively. The plot was hard to follow without an understanding of its background, which was disclosed by Helms in his 15 December 1987 Senate speech. Actually though, the show was part of a political indoctrination program, designed to condition the audience for acceptance of a new order. As Helms explains: "A careful examination of what is happening behind the scenes reveals that all of these interests [i.e., "the Department of State, the Department of Commerce, the money center banks and multinational corporations, the media, the educational establishment, the entertainment industry, and the large tax-exempt foundations"] are working in concert with the masters of the Kremlin in order to create what some refer to as a new world order." Helms continues:

> Private organizations such as the Council on Foreign Relations, the Royal Institute of International Affairs, the Trilateral Commission, the Dartmouth Conference, the Aspen Institute of Humanistic Studies, the Atlantic Institute, and the Bilderberg group serve to disseminate and to coordinate the plans for this so-called new world order in powerful business, financial, academic, and official circles.[103]

Reagan's role in this show, unlike that of "the great Gipper," was a duplicitous president known as "the great Gypper." However, being a puppet, he had two heads, which were alternately screwed off and on. Gorbachev, the co-star, had only one head, but with two faces on it, one smiling and the other veiled.

As in the videotape, Act I begins with Gorby sauntering down a long red carpet at the Washington airport while being greeted by thousands of flag-waving dupes—Soviet flags! Then, on his way to the Red—uh,

White House, he is seen smiling at the large red flag (having a yellow hammer and sickle with a star above them), which adorns it. His other eyes, peering over the veil, are fixed on those "alongside the Stars and Stripes on the lampposts across the street."[104] Suddenly, we are shown a busy street in Washington where hordes of vendors are shamelessly pushing their Gorbachev T-shirts, Lenin pins, summit buttons, postcards, and, of course, Soviet flags. These flags are everywhere. As one critic describes it:

> The sight of all the Russian flags in Washington sickened me! Some were even flown on the same flagpole with the hammer and sickle <u>ABOVE</u> the stars and stripes! Never before has the bloody Soviet flag been shown on an equal basis with our flag. Did you see the flags behind Reagan and Gorbachev at the signing of the treaty? What a terrible symbolic picture this will make for the remaining anti-Communist people and nations.

> While I was watching some of the TV coverage of this "Red Love-in" starring Ron and Gorby, I had a feeling that I was watching the real version of the TV show "Amerika. . . ."[105]

Later, in Act I, we get a close-up of the Gyp wearing a set of gold cuff links. Their design shows the prophet Isaiah beating swords into plow-shares (Isa. 2:4). Next, since he just happens to have an extra set, he gives it to Gorby, who is noticeably confused. Then, pointing to the design, the Gyp tearfully associates it with the INF treaty and "world peace," as Gorby smilingly scratches his head. Apparently, neither of them realize that, as prophesied, though there will be world peace, it won't be due to the efforts of men.

As the curtain opens on Act II, we see the Gyp with an arm around Gorby (who is watching it from beneath his veil). Then, smiling at each other deferentially, they begin to stroll about Red Square. They are very happy because of the U.S. Senate's ratification of the INF treaty. However, agreeing that much more could be done, they agree to sign more agreements.

We also see that the Gyp is proudly sporting a neat-looking lapel pin with two crossed flags on it, one which is very, very red. A close-up shows they are those of the U.S. and the U.S.S.R., implying that the Gyp equates Old Glory with Old Gory. As the action unfolds, we notice that this pinko propaganda pin is on him everywhere. Whether tramping about Red Square, twiddling with Gorby, or twaddling at Moscow State, it is there. Finally, during a stop-over in London on his way home (still flaunting his pin), the Gyp is shown gushing at the Guildhall:

> To those of us who remember the postwar era, all of this is cause for shaking the head in wonder. Imagine the President of the United States and the General Secretary of the Soviet Union walking together in Red Square, talking about a growing personal friendship.[106]

This obviously is not the 1980 Reagan, or is it? Could this one have been hiding behind a facade, pretending to be what he wasn't? If not, which one is real? And how can the difference between them be explained? By 1988, during the Moscow summit, he and Gorbachev were "walking together in Red Square, talking about a growing personal friendship." In 1980, this would have been unimaginable—or if predicted, "cause for shaking the head in wonder."

Yet, to most Americans, Reagan was still how they saw him in 1980. They simply couldn't "believe that a Republican could be 'soft on Communism' or would jeopardize our liberty or sovereignty,"[107] especially Reagan. They had long been conditioned, since his Hollywood days, to believe that he was a diehard anti-Communist, even an FBI informer.[108] He was that all-American boy—like in the movies: mom, apple pie, and all that stuff, oh, and a patriotic World War II vet—or sort of. Besides, he had promised, with tears in his eyes, to "make America great again"—which he would have, bewail the Reaganuts, if only we had given him the kind of "Congress he needed."[109] Yes, it's all our fault.

Even the watchdogs, with several exceptions, were still asleep, oblivious to the red glow at the end of their dark tunnels. Two exceptions were Howard Phillips and Richard Viguerie. Having been awakened by the strange sound of what appeared to be a papier mâché eagle cooing, they decided to investigate. For they had also noticed the red glow. Soon, to their horror, they were gazing upon the abomination of abominations: a two-headed pink dove posing as an eagle having an unnatural relationship with a two-faced, red vulture (partially veiled) posing as a dove. There was also false shrieking and cooing. Then, to the ritualistic chanting and beating of drums, they did the "perestroika waltz," while around them the earth was on fire.

That is, turned off by Reagan's adulation of the Kremliniks, including his maudlin fawning over Gorbachev, Phillips called him a "useful idiot" while Viguerie labeled him an "apologist for Gorbachev."[110] Reagan had claimed, during the Washington summit that the Soviet Union had changed, that today's "Soviet leaders [don't accept] the Marxian theory of the one-world Communist state."[111] They are therefore now opposed to establishing Marxist-Leninist regimes around the world, which is exactly what they were doing while he was saying this.

He also said Gorbachev "is looking for a situation [wherein we can live] peacefully together in the world."[112] And he is, of course. The Soviets have always sought "world peace," which, they admit, is inseparable from communism. As Afanasiev put it, "the struggle for communism . . . is intrinsically bound up with the struggle for peace in the world."[113] So what's new? Why did

Reagan ignore this? Was it intentional? Probably, for he also ignored Gorbachev's 2 November 1987 statement: "We are moving toward a new world, the world of communism. We shall never turn off that road."[114]

This "world of communism" then must be the "situation [wherein we can live] peacefully together in the world" especially since, about two years later, he said, "I am a Communist. I shall remain a convinced one . . . for me it is a goal."[115] Thus, as Gorbachev implies (and as Reagan must have known), communism *is not* dead. Nor have the Soviets really changed. It's still business as usual. And any perceived changes are merely manifestations of the "new phase in Soviet-American relations," or "detente offensive." After all, the Soviets are now in the pre-convergence stage, awaiting "construction of a global political condominium by [U.S.] financiers and the Kremlin,"[116] which brings us back to Bush's "new world" or Solodovnikov's "socialist (Communist) community."[117]

So, what was Reagan up to? Was his agenda the same as Bush's, which concerned "[preparation] for the new world"?[118] Apparently it was, though it wasn't really his. It was Rocky-Bye's—those who were pulling his strings, such as, perhaps, Bush. Imperceptibly. Or are we to believe that Bush was patiently waiting for eight years to do what he could have done then? And that Rocky-Bye had postponed its agenda, while allowing Reagan to carry out his own, even though he didn't have one.

To pull strings though, Bush would have had to be close to Reagan, and intimately involved in White House operations. Such an arrangement, it seems, would have been unlikely, considering they were once political rivals. Right? Wrong. With Reagan, the unlikely was often likely, which is why, after winning the primaries "he pledged that Bush, unlike other vice presidents, would play an important role in his administration. Reagan followed through on that pledge, drawing Bush deep into the inner sanctums, virtually letting him sit by his side as he conducted his presidency."[119]

This, of course, isn't the whole picture. He was also encompassed by 313 of Bush's colleagues from the Council on Foreign Relations,[120] and a bunch of Trilateralists. But he liked these insiders and "longed to be part of [them.]"[121] There was one problem though. They were somewhat under Bush. That is, besides being vice-president, he was the acting president, unofficially. So where did this leave Reagan? Well, as author Antony Sutton explained during Reagan's second term, ". . . Reagan prefers a relaxed management style leaving policy and its implementation to subordinates . . . and Bush is the senior of these subordinates. This places Bush in an unusually good position to take over the reins."[122] And did he? He sure did. "In fact," notes investigative journalist Joel Bainerman, "far from being a wimp, George Bush ran the White House. Says former Army investigator Gene Wheaton: 'Ronald Reagan may have been President but George Bush was in charge.'" Bainerman continues:

> Bush was smart. He figured out that to implement his secret agendas all he had to do was arrange it so he was appointed chairman of all the important White House committees [e.g., Task Force on Combating Terrorism]. *This meant he could appoint the key people to work on these interagency committees to establish policy and [his] covert agendas* [emphasis mine].[123]

Reagan's "relaxed [or passive] management" was management only in the term's loosest definition. As one White House insider described it, "[Reagan] made no demands, and gave almost no instructions. [He] just responded to whatever was brought to his attention and said yes or no, or I'll think about it."[124] That's management?! And what if it wasn't "brought to his attention"? Well, then, says the insider, "Reagan [was] helpless—

and disaster [could] strike."[125] He adds: "This [was] particularly true for matters where much of the information [was] secret . . . and there [was] no normal press coverage,"[126] such as Rocky Bye's agenda. For what could be more secret? And what would get less press coverage? Besides, he was in no way inimical to it.

So what was Reagan doing? Whatever he was told or conditioned to do. And he didn't have to think since he had people to do it for him. Foreign policy, for example, was handled by Rocky-Bye-Baby, via his CFR-controlled "foreign policy directorate."[127] Apparently Bush was its most influential member since, besides Casey and Weinberger, he "was the only member of the directorate who was there from the beginning." Moreover, he "went to all the important meetings, met regularly with the president for private weekly lunches, and was intimately tied to the entire foreign policy community. He was everywhere, but he left few visible tracks, sometimes not even finger prints."[128]

Reagan didn't have to think about domestic policy either, for much the same reason. Except that it was determined by the CFR-dominated "cabinet councils," of which Bush was an ex officio member. They also included Trilateralist David Stockman (Office of Management and Budget) and Murray Weidenbaum (Council of Economic Advisers), both CFR members.[129] Then what was left for him to think about? Nothing of any importance. Not even the White House? Nope. That was run by Nancy and Deaver, as author Kitty Kelley explains:

> Deaver was part of the inner circle because he had made himself indispensable to Mrs. Reagan, who worked her will through his accommodating manner. Together, they presided over the White House, dictating the President's schedule, shaping his policies, and choosing his personnel, including his ambassadors. Together, they rewarded their friends and punished their enemies.[130]

Carrying out Bush's "new world" agenda under Reagan was a piece of cake, not just because of his non-management style but also because of Reagan himself—superstitions, good luck charms, daily horoscopes, and jelly beans.[131] A liberal aide and "a power-hungry, image-obsessed [wife] who, guided by astrologers, ran the White House."[132] A professed Christian who, after many years, still couldn't fathom the Lord's Supper.[133] A man who, according to a Carnegie Mellon professor, "lacks both the intellectual and emotional stature to fill the position into which providence had cast him." Furthermore: "[Reagan] has little real grasp of affairs, shows frequent laziness, and suffers above all from an inability to deal forcefully with anyone around him."[134]

This doesn't mean that Reagan is stupid. After all, wasn't he an Army officer during World War II, and therefore had to have at least 120 on the Army General Classification Test (AGCT), and a high mechanical aptitude? Well, yes, he was an officer, a reservist called up for wartime duty. But he may not have taken these tests. Even certain physical requirements were waived in his case. That is, he was restricted to "limited service" only.[135]

Yet, more important than how well he thinks is what he thinks, and why. Including why he tends to be duplicitous, and so naturally, seemingly without conscience—like one dedicated to a revolutionary cause, some amorphous, utopian concept, such as "world peace" or the "kingdom of God," believing that any means for attaining it, even communism, is reasonable and just, for God said so.

Reagan is enigmatic, being worldly and ambitious, but also religious, having many idols. He's like the gracious, fatherly mafian chieftain who prays every night for wisdom and guidance, and the souls of his victims, sacrificed on the altar of expediency. But Reagan had a dream—in color. There was this pie in the sky on which everyone lived in peace. And there was a bear lying down with an eagle.

So what makes Reagan tick? What have we yet to learn about him—and where would we go to find it? Well, what about his alma mater, Eureka College? Where he still goes—to find himself—the real Ronald Reagan.

TWO

Peace, Peace, Peace

Eureka College is in Eureka, Illinois, about eighty miles south of Reagan's hometown, Dixon, and twenty miles east of Peoria. Eureka, a town of about 2,000, is surrounded by corn and pumpkin fields; and alongside the two highways leading into it are official green and white signs reading:

EUREKA COLLEGE
ALMA MATER OF
PRESIDENT RONALD W. REAGAN

The school, about midtown, is as lifeless as the cemetery that adjoins it. This cemetery, which is separated from the campus by a narrow road called Reagan Drive, is the one Reagan mentions in his autobiography, *Ronald Reagan's Own Story*: "[Finding] privacy for philosophic discussions and such always presented a problem. Local geography contributed to Eureka's traditional solution for this problem—the cemetery was a three-minute walk from the campus. Everyone had his favorite grave . . . with a . . . tombstone [for] a backrest. . . ."[1]

Almost as dead is the town itself, its most prominent features being the water tower, a muddy pond, and an abandoned movie theatre . . . oh, and the empty buildings where the highways meet and pot holes . . . the rusty pickup truck . . . a stray cat. Nothing is more bleak than Eureka on a cold winter night—the snow blowing over the campus and through the cemetery.

Facing north on the left of the cross made by the highways is the Eureka Christian Church (Disciples of

Christ), an affiliate of the National/ World Council of Churches (NCC/WCC), which is why the town was merged with a Soviet town called Elan. This is the church Reagan and his girlfriend, Margaret Cleaver, attended. Her father was the minister. He had previously pastored the Disciples church in Dixon, of which Reagan was a member. He reminisces:

> [My] hero had been the . . . son of the minister Margaret's father was later to replace. He went to Eureka College, where . . . he starred in football. I had never seen Eureka College but it was my choice. I don't know what might have happened if Margaret had chosen another school, but I didn't have that problem to face. Her older sisters had gone to Eureka and she was slated to go there too, probably because of her father and the fact that Eureka was a Christian Church college. . . .[2]

Near the school's main entrance is Melick Library where the Ronald Reagan Memorabilia Collection is housed. Visitors have access to more than 800 items from his movie, television, and political careers, along with a wide variety of biographical material. Across the street, but set way back, is Pritchard Hall, the Fine Arts Center, which Reagan and his brother, Neil, remember as a gymnasium in the 1930s.

The school is intimately associated with Reagan's outlook on life.[3] It is the setting of many of his most cherished memories. During his 1980 visit, while campaigning, he said, "This is a place that lives in your heart."[4] Thus, being emotionally attached to the school, he has been involved in its affairs since graduating in 1932. He even became a trustee, completing three six-year terms: 1947-53, 1967-73, and 1974-80.[5] Following his last term, Neil, a 1933 graduate, took over.

The school's history has not been one of growth. It had only about 250 students when Reagan arrived in 1928—or, as he put it, "roughly 130 boys and 120 girls, enough to make any sex competition interesting,"[6] which was the same as in 1882.[7] A hundred years later, in 1982, there were only about 265 more, or 515. That year marked the 50th anniversary of Reagan's graduation, an occasion he used for a major foreign policy address.[8]

Eureka's president then was Daniel D. Gilbert, an ordained Disciples minister. Though he was usually called "Dr. Gilbert," his only doctorate was an honorary one from Lynchburg College, Virginia, another Disciples institution, where he got his B.A. His "doctorate" was awarded in May 1977, after he became president in April.[9]

During Gilbert's eight years as president, Reagan visited the school four times: 1979, 1980, 1982, and 1984. Gilbert "[served] on his transition committee, and [also] as a member of [his] Task Force on Private Sector Initiatives."[10] In 1982, Gilbert officially launched the Ronald W. Reagan Scholarship Program.[11] This program, which honored Reagan, possibly had something to do with Eureka's National Advisory Council. As one of the trustees that founded the council in 1979, Reagan became its chairman. Its purpose is "to strengthen the College academically and financially."[12]

Research covering Gilbert's last four years (coincidental with Reagan's first term) suggests that the school was unstable. Many of its dorm students, for instance, had alcohol problems. This led to rule-breaking, since alcohol was prohibited. Gilbert saw this ban as being "unenforceable," probably because of his sympathy for, or empathy with, the rule-breakers: "It's very difficult for them to arrive here, having been used to drinking, and then be told that they're not allowed to drink . . . ." He therefore didn't want to punish them, which created a dilemma: a choice between punishing them or ignoring the problem. So he ignored the problem, but under the guise of solving it through "edjoocay-shun." He explained: "We need to educate the students on the difficulties involved with alcohol and other drugs. We'll be spending a lot of time educationally rather than disciplinary . . . ."[13]

Another problem was the school's emphasis on the student's psychological well-being, which was conflictive with its primary function: by definition, to provide instruction. At least one teacher knew this, complaining at a faculty meeting that degrees at Eureka "were largely fraudulent." That is, "most graduates can neither read nor write." Adding: "[Students often maneuver through their programs] without taking a single course [requiring] them to think."[14]

Most of Eureka's problems, it seems, were related to its inherent, or built-in, mediocrity. So enshrined was it that any legitimate attempt to pursue academic excellence was likely to be seen as threatening to the status quo. This discouraged innovation and contributed to job insecurity, particularly among new teachers already demoralized by the school's shortage of funds, low salaries, and precarious contract-tenure system.

The faculty and staff, generally speaking, seemed cynical and impassive. There was therefore a lack of human warmth, accompanied by a nebulous feeling of ill-will. This unfriendliness, of course, excluded the symbiotic relationships within the various cliques, the most influential of them being the one associated with the Christian Church (Disciples of Christ), which "[maintained] close ties" with the school.[15] This group's chief interest, it seems, was the promotion of the NCC/ WCC complex's left-wing agenda.

Even the town itself was affected by this agenda, which was associated with the Disciples' Shalom Congregation Program. For example, through one of the program's satellite groups, the Eureka Peace Issues Council (EPIC), Eureka was "paired with a town in Russia called Elan."[16] Along with an official greeting from Eureka's mayor, packets of information on Eureka's schools, factories, medical facilities, etc., were sent to Elan, which, of course, ended up in the KGB's files.

The Shalom program was developed in 1980 by some education specialists in St. Louis. It began as a pilot project consisting of ten churches, which were to include the idea of "peace-making" in their worship services, studies, and community activities. Each of these churches was committed to send a representative to the 1981 Riverside Church Disarmament Conference in New York. This meeting is mentioned in *The Coercive Utopians:* "Themes that Soviet fronts like the World Peace Council and the Christian Peace Conference have emphasized for years, that the only alternative to peace . . . is annihilation, have swept through the peace movement . . . . A Riverside Church Disarmament Conference in November 1981 warned:

> "We're on the brink of extinction." In the past, pacifist movements always faced the problem of convincing the public that pacifism was a viable way to obtain national security. Even the moral case was ambiguous, for it meant abstention from force when an aggressor ravished a peaceful country. But now, the [choice] is presented as being between nuclear disarmament and nuclear holocaust.[17]

One of the churches in the pilot project was the Eureka Christian church, represented by Clarence and Charlotte Noe. Clarence, a 1938 Eureka College graduate, was a retired Eureka dean and psychology professor.[18] His wife, Charlotte, was a Eureka trustee.[19] According to the Disciples' journal, *The Disciple:*

> Clarence and Charlotte Noe were sent [to the conference] by their congregation from the home of Eureka (Illinois) College, where President Ronald Reagan graduated. . . . Upon their return, they started slowly and gently, working the focus on peacemaking into the church's classrooms, sanctuary, and local outreach.[20]

The year of the conference, 1981, was the same year Eureka awarded Clarence Noe an honorary doctorate.[21] It was also the year Reagan's brother Neil became a trustee. Following this conference, the Noes became co-chairmen of the Eureka Christian Church's Shalom committee. Reporting on their church's 1983-84 Shalom activities, they write:

> Last August . . . representatives of our church appeared in nine Cluster churches and made a . . . presentation . . . in observance of Hiroshima Day . . .

> Peace Sunday was observed on December 4, with the sermon, litany and music focusing on our concern for peace. The film "Gods of Metal" [sic] was shown during Adult Study. . . .

> The committee discussed the need for a position paper on "Peace with Justice." Dr. Humbert . . . presented a statement for committee discussion . . . at the March meeting.

> From this meeting came the idea for a "Shalom Celebration" to initiate peace week observance at the May Fellowship Potluck. A skit was prepared and focused on . . . ways in which the congregation . . . is giving witness to Shalom. Program possibilities for next year were . . . Parenting for Peace, Focus on Central America, and Partners in Shalom. . . .

> Memorial Day Sunday was observed as Peace Sunday. . . .

> The committee was instrumental in establishing EPIC (Eureka Peace Issues Council) last Fall. . . . Through EPIC, Eureka is paired with a town in Russia called Elan.[22]

The Christian Church (Disciples of Christ) is relatively unknown. This seems odd since, besides having over a million members, its most famous one is Reagan, who, says *The Disciple*, "grew up in our church."[23] This is because his mother, Nelle, who was "an active member of the Disciples of Christ," had "a powerful influence on [him.]"[24] He had even "performed in church plays with [her];" and later, "as an adult, he accompanied her to church services regularly, even giving [the church] a percentage of his weekly income. . . ."[25] Also, in 1952, he and Nancy were married in a Disciples church.[26] He was still a Eureka trustee then. This was not long after Nancy's "name kept showing up on rosters of Communist front organizations."[27]

In contrast, the Disciples can also be identified by their most infamous member, Jim Jones, a Disciples minister. Though his church, the People's Temple, was in San Francisco, he formed a commune in Guyana, called Jonestown. Later, in 1978, he led over 900 of his followers to their deaths in a mass suicide ritual, using a fruit-flavored drink spiked with cyanide.

Most of the explanations for Jones's behavior were psychological. They were, in a sense, excuses, portraying him as a victim rather than an evildoer. We read in *The Disciple*, for instance: "Jim Jones' wife told the *New York Times* in 1977 that he once threw down the Bible with great energy and exclaimed, 'Marcie, I've got to destroy this paper idol.' That seems to be where he had gone wrong, taking his people with him—so closely identifying himself with God that he ultimately tried to take the place of God, finally destroying what goodness he had accomplished along the way."[28]

Such psychological analyses ignore the fact that Jones's sanity had never been questioned before. Like Reagan, he was well-liked and much respected. "[He] had been appointed to . . . government commissions, and even [received] a letter of commendation from . . . Rosalyn Carter."[29] In 1975, he was recognized by "a national interfaith organization . . . as one of the hundred most outstanding clergymen in [America.]"[30] So why wasn't his behavior simply thought of as being evil?

Author Herbert Schlossberg (*Idols for Destruction*) notes that

> psychiatrist Thomas Szasz searched the whole literature on the incident and found that universally the politicians, journalists, lawyers, psychiatrists, and other experts had concluded that Jones was insane. . . .Yet Szasz could find no evidence that anyone had doubted Jones' sanity before the incident. In fact, a gala fundraising dinner in his honor, endorsed by seventy-five prominent leaders, was scheduled in San Francisco for December 2, 1978, and had to be cancelled after the massacre. Szasz's explanation makes more sense than any of the pundits and experts: "I think he was an evil man."[31]

Perhaps these "experts" were psychological because "they no longer believed, if they ever had, that evil acts are done by evil people."[32] This may also be why *The Disciple* saw Jones's behavior as having more to do with Freudian psychology than "spiritual wickedness in high places,"[33] which is possibly due to the denomination's faith in secular education—and indifference to Biblically-based doctrine.

That is, as they see it, Scripture may be interpreted according to one's own fancies. This though results in false theological systems, especially when influenced by such secular disciplines as philosophy, literature, and the behavioral sciences. Mystical concepts from the Eastern religions, for instance, lead to New Ageism (i.e., spiritual humanism).[34] A Disciples minister describes this doctrinal anarchy:

> So whether you believe in the literal interpretation of all Scripture is not a test in a Disciples congregation. Whether you believe in the trinity, angels, demons, . . . predestination, or whatever—these matters are left up to us. The only essential question is: Do you believe that Jesus is the Christ, the Son of God?

> The implication . . . is that we must think seriously about what we believe. We have no creed to define the faith with finality for everyone; we have no catechism. So we must work out our own faith . . . . Some of us, reacting to our freedom of theology, have no theology at all.[35]

This "doctrine of no doctrine" is evident in a Disciples brochure called *Characteristic Beliefs of the Christian Church,* which suggests that its beliefs can be found in the somewhat poetic "Preamble of the Design for the Christian Church (Disciples of Christ)."[36] The brochure itself is little more than a summary of the "poem." While it mentions certain well-known Christian beliefs and rites, it does so ambiguously (and superficially), perhaps to facilitate freedom of interpretation.

Much of this confusion can probably be traced to the denomination's founders themselves, particularly Barton W. Stone (1772-1844) and Thomas Campbell (1763-1854). Because of Stone and Campbell, it seems, the Disciples are still obsessed with church unification. That is, bringing all of the denominations together in spite of their conflicting doctrinal positions. Campbell once proclaimed that "the church . . . is essentially, intentionally, and constitutionally one" and that "division among Christians is a horrid evil."[37] Also, says a Disciples minister, "Stone and Campbell even varied in their attitudes toward the Trinity." Whereas "Stone found the doctrine of the Trinity neither sensible nor biblical," Campbell found it "difficult to understand." Actually, he

> objected to any kind of doctrine in the Christian Church, whether it be the doctrine of the Trinity, or a doctrine of the virgin birth, or any other doctrine. And I would guess that this is probably the greatest reason we Disciples have demurred when it comes to the doctrine of the Trinity . . . i.e., because we have always claimed to be non-doctrinal.[38]

The Disciples are also confused about the Millennium (i.e., the thousand-year reign of Christ).[39] Though it is prophesied that Christ will return following the Great Tribulation to usher in the millennial age, the Disciples, apparently, plan to bring it in themselves. Thus many of them confuse the Millennium with Rocky-Bye-Baby's new world order. This may be why Reagan gave Gorbachev the set of gold cuff links "[depicting the] prophet Isaiah breaking swords into plowshares."[40] Even Campbell's son, Alexander, envisioned a new order, which he associated with Christ's return:

> Alexander Campbell looked in expectation to the conversion of the world in preparation for Christ's kingdom. . . . His view of the millennium, however, was not other-worldly; it was a vision based upon this world and included a wide range of social, political, and moral concerns.[41]

This may be why the Disciples—one of the WCC's most pacifistic denominations—are so zealously pushing the "social gospel" or, in their words, bringing "the gospel message to bear upon the life of the world, especially in the elimination of all injustice, discrimination, and poverty"[42] and why they're supportive of the United Nations. In his 1986 UN address, for instance, Reagan claimed that the UN arose from a "devotion to the dream of world peace and freedom, of human rights and democratic self-determination," which he probably believed. He also said: "[It] has provided an international forum for harmonizing conflicting national interests and has made a significant contribution in such fields as peace-keeping, humanitarian assistance, and eradicating disease."[43]

However, most significant was his reference to the mysterious UN Meditation Room, which, according to former UN honcho Dag Hammarskjold, represented "the unity of all world religions."[44] Hammarskjold, a Socialist, was "imbued with an exaggerated, humanistic view of his ability to 'save the world.' " He even thought of himself as "a new Jesus."[45] This though didn't keep Reagan from quoting him (Hammarskjold's remark during the Room's construction in 1957): "We want to bring back the idea of worship . . . devotion to something which is greater and higher than we are ourselves." Soon after, author John F. McManus wrote:

> Incredible! The UN has always gone out of its way to ignore God totally. It constructed a cubicle featuring a stone slab and a small mural chock full of occult symbols, dubbed it the "Meditation Room," and postured about it being the equivalent of a truly religious chapel. Sadly, the President of the United States swallowed the entire fraud—hook, line and mural.[46]

Perhaps by "devotion to something . . . greater and higher," Reagan had the stars in mind. His former White House chief of staff, Donald T. Regan, says: "Virtually every major move or decision the Reagans made . . . was cleared in advance with [astrologer Joan Quigley] who drew up horoscopes to make certain that the planets were in favorable alignment . . . ."[47] This though should have been expected. Regan, and his fellow insiders, must have known that, back in the early fifties, Reagan was getting "career advice from [Carroll] Righter," the Hollywood astrologer. So why the surprise?

But that's not all. "By the '60s, Reagan's interest had turned to politics, and his stable of advisors had widened to include Jeane Dixon."[48] Also included was Sybil Leek, the English witch. Following her advice, Reagan was sworn in as California's thirty-third governor "right after midnight facing west."[49]

Meanwhile, Reagan was still seeing Righter, a homosexual. Privately, it had been reported in the *New York Post* "that 'a homosexual ring had been operating out of Governor Reagan's office for six months with his full knowledge. . . ."[50] Nancy, of course, was seeing Righter, too, visiting him regularly at his "sprawling Hollywood Hills mansion." All this, hypocritically, after Reagan had publicly "condemned [homosexuality] as 'an abomination in the eyes of the Lord.' "[51] But so is astrology, which is why it's forbidden.[52] As for Nancy, Kitty Kelley notes: "[While] her mother-in-law placed her faith in God, Nancy placed hers in astrology. Nelle Reagan studied the Bible; her daughter-in-law read tea leaves."[53]

Though the Reagans might not know it, astrology is an occult science, and is associated with ancient Babylon's religion: worship of the Mother Goddess (Ishtar). This goddess "was the original Virgo of the Zodiac signs . . . ."[54] In Texe Marrs's *Mystery Mark of the New Age,* we learn: "To many in today's New Age Movement, the symbol of Virgo—and in fact the entire field of astrology—has profound religious significance." And in Virgo's case, it is *very, very* profound. In what way? Well, says Marrs, "Virgo, the goddess, is acknowledged as represented numerologically by three 6s; 666 is her number—the number of the Beast." So does this mean she'll be the Antichrist? No. Marrs explains that she simply represents "the ungodly worldwide religious system he will head: Mystery, Babylon . . . . From this perverse New Age Mystery Religion will spring forth a son. He will be Satan in the form of a man: a Man-Beast who leads a religious Beast system. He will be the Antichrist who rules and terrorizes a tribulation-plagued world."[55]

It's not surprising then that Reagan, like Carter and Bush, is also a Freemason. He became an honorary thirty-three degree (Scottish Rite) just "before his second term of office was completed."[56] But what's Freemasonry got to do with New Ageism? Just one thing. There's not a farthing's worth of difference between them. For example, they have the same god, Lucifer, and the same goal, a new world order. They also practice occultism, using the same occult symbols such as the pentagram, hexagram, triangle, circle, ankh, sun, moon, stars, serpent, pyramid, and all-seeing eye.

Moreover, as sun worshippers, both Masons and New Agers identify with light, or illumination, even calling themselves "children of light." Masonic writer Foster Bailey (New Ager Alice Bailey's spouse), for instance, reveals that the Masters of Wisdom gradually "assist at the unfolding of the consciousness of the candidate until the time comes when he can 'enter into light,' and in his turn become a LIGHT-BEARER, one of the ILLUMINATI who can assist the Lodge on High in bringing humanity to light." These terms are defined by Dr. Cathy Burns (*Hidden Secrets of Masonry*): "[The] word 'LUCIFER' means 'LIGHT BEARER,' so Masons are the 'children of light' or, actually, 'the children of LUCIFER.' " Also, she says,

> The "Masters of Wisdom" are spirit guides (actually DEMONS) who are supposedly directing the way to a ONE WORLD ORDER and the ILLU-MINATI is an organization that was founded on May 1, 1776 by Adam Weishaupt. The name "Illuminati" is derived from Lucifer. The Illuminati was dedicated to a "NEW WORLD ORDER" or a "ONE WORLD GOVERNMENT"—the EXACT goal of the NEW AGERS today.[57]

Spirit guides? Demons? Do such things really exist? Well, yes, according to the Bible (1 Tim. 4:1): "[In] the latter times some shall depart from the faith, giving heed to seducing spirits, and doctrines of devils [i.e., demons, or fallen angels]." Are they in any way associated with astrology? They sure are. After all, its purpose (as in "tea leaf reading, runes, fortune-telling, and palmistry") is to acquire "information through occult means." This, explains former New Age leader Randall N. Baer, opens the door for "demons to subtly weave their works, oftentimes in invisible, devious ways." However, he says, some "astrologers . . . would deny [being] in contact with any spirits whatsoever in rendering a person's astrological chart interpretation." Baer quotes John Ankerberg and John Weldon (*The Facts on the New Age Movement*): " '[The] teachings of the New Age are the teachings of spirits. What the New Age teaches and believes is what the spirit world has revealed and wishes men to believe . . .' "[58]

Still, belief in astrology is not, it seems, incompatible with the Disciples' "doctrine of no doctrine" since, tautologically, such a doctrine would be open to all doctrine. This would include, of course, the various philosophical isms such as communism, Illuminism, and New Ageism, all of which are pantheistic. They are also collectivistic and therefore share a common objective: "world peace" (i.e., world government).

That Reagan was receptive to Bahaism then is understandable. Bahaism, having its origin in Babism, is also pantheistic, collectivistic, and peace-seeking. His interest in it began during his relationship with actress Christine Larson, "a devout Bahai," with whom "he was deeply in love." Whenever she talked about Bahaism, he "was very moved," and possibly attended "Bahai firesides" with her. One of Larson's Bahai friends felt this was why Reagan later "issued a public statement calling for a halt to the execution of Bahais in Iran."

All of this occurred while Reagan was attending the Hollywood Beverly Christian Church with his mother. Yet, says Kitty Kelley, it was because of his mother's religious zeal that he was so "receptive to [Larson's] commitment." "As a Bahai," she writes, "[Larson] believed Bahaullah to be the most recent in the line of Messengers of God, a line that included Abraham, Moses, Buddha, Zoroaster, Jesus, and Muhammad. One of the fundamental objectives of the Bahai faith is establishing world peace within the framework of a unified, spiritually enlightened new world order."[59]

A "spiritually enlightened new world order"? But this is what Rocky-Bye-Baby and the Communists want.

The New Agers also want it. And what about the National/World Council of Churches, including the Disciples? Isn't this their kingdom of God, a "spiritually enlightened" global Jonestown?

Few realize that, prior to Jonestown, Jones's People's Temple was a New Age church.[60] And that Jones was a Communist. This is why the Disciples find the subject of Jonestown embarrassing, and why they try to avoid it. Thus, like Rocky-Bye's propaganda mill, they employ the "Pinsky Principle," named after Walter Pinsky, the writer who admitted that journalists, including himself, keep silent to avoid "red baiting." An example of this, write Rael and Erich Isaac (*The Coercive Utopians*), "was the failure of CBS in its two-part drama, *Guyana Tragedy: The Story of Jim Jones*, to say a word concerning Jones as a Communist.

> Jones had broken with the U.S. Communist Party, according to his own account, because it had turned against Stalin and "I loved Stalin." Nonetheless, his feelings toward the party had clearly mellowed, for his will provided that in the absence of immediate surviving family, his estate should go to the U.S. Communist Party. Jones had also ordered that $7 million [tithings?] belonging to the People's Temple be transferred to the Soviet Union.[61]

Besides believing the utopians, the Isaacs say, the media protects them. Whatever embarrasses them is "simply not reported."[62] Thus Reagan was able to pose as a conservative even after admitting he was "an active (though unconscious) partisan in what now and then turned out to be Communist causes . . . ."[63] That is, having joined a Communist front organization after the war, he "became a large wheel in their operations."[64] But the media doesn't want us to know this. So they ignore it, or provide excuses for it, psychological ones, as in Jones's case. Yet, it has never been questioned as to how a 35-year-old, ex-Army Air Corps captain could have been so imprudent.

Reagan also admits (for some reason) that, prior to their marriage, Nancy "was very much distressed because her name kept showing up on rosters of Communist front organizations." He says "her mail frequently included notices of meetings she had no desire to attend, and accounts of these meetings as covered by the *Daily Worker*."[65] However, he assures us, it was just a mistake. There was really nothing to it. That's it. Case closed.

Then, in early '52, they were married. He was near the end of his first term (1947-1953) as a Eureka trustee. (And, for some reason, he waited until 1967 before beginning his second one, 1967-1973.) Shortly after, during McCarthy's hearings, Bob Hope quipped:

> It is wonderful in the spring to watch the birds teaching their young to fly . . . and I saw my first robin bluebreast the other day. They changed from redbreast out here . . . they were afraid they might get investigated.[66]

Notwithstanding ultralib Michael Deaver's closeness to Nancy, his *Behind the Scenes* reveals little about her views (or Reagan's) on communism. This, natch, is typical of the "liberal" mind wherein truth is hidden or inverted, thus, the "Pinsky Principle." While Deaver mentions Jonestown, he falsely associates it with "the 'Jim Jones Wing' of the Republican Party, those willing to prove their loyalty by drinking the spiked Kool-Aid."[67]

Yet, he does quote director John Huston, who knew her well, as saying, "The idea that Nancy is an archconservative and reactionary [i.e., one opposed to liberalism] and that she is the influence on Ronnie and guided his political thinking is absurd, absolute nonsense." He was right, of course, since Reagan was just like her. Deaver adds: "[Rather than moving Reagan] to the right, Nancy [persuaded] him to take the longer view of history. When [he was asked] to get tough with the Soviets, she argued that he should soften his language."

Still, says Deaver, she knew he "was a man [of] peace."[68] She even confirms this herself: "[Soviet foreign minister Gromyko] turned to me and said, 'Is your husband for peace or war?' And I said, 'Peace' . . . He was a little bit surprised . . . and he said, 'You sure?' And I said, 'Yes.' . . . He turned to me and said, 'You whisper peace into his ear every night.' And I said, 'Oh, I will. And I'll also whisper peace in your ear.' "[69] What did they mean by "peace"? Deaver provides a clue: "She lobbied the president to soften his line on the Soviet Union; to reduce military spending and not to push Star Wars at the expense of the poor and dispossessed. She favored a diplomatic solution in Nicaragua . . ."[70]

Deaver mentions his lunch with Marxist playwright Lillian Hellman and columnist Joseph Alsop (CFR). He says "Nancy Reagan would have enjoyed that lunch."[71] However, he leaves us uncertain as to why. He merely says it gave her a chance to meet "people with diverse views." Also, he implies, it would have gotten her out of the house. But, according to Kelley, she was in no way bored or in need of company. Hellman, who was "a long-time Communist party member . . . left part of her $4 million estate for the creation of a fund for Marxist writers to be named after Dashiell Hammett," a Communist with whom she lived.[72]

Deaver uses the lunch to depict Reagan as being fiercely anti-Communist, the opposite of Hellman. "When I [mentioned Hellman]," says Deaver, "[Reagan] was puzzled, almost angry. 'Lillian Hellman!' he said. 'Dammit, she still thinks Joe Stalin is great,' "[73] thus innocence through dissociation.

Reagan's own defense against charges of pinkishness is usually feigned naivete, such as playing dumb and then laughing things off. What does he know about communism? Nothing, of course. As he put it: "I knew little and cared less about the rumors about Communists." He adds, "I was truly so naive I thought the nearest Communists were fighting in Stalingrad."[74]

This is like saying he was unaware of William Z. Foster or Earl Browder, two notorious Communists known to most Americans born around 1911, Reagan's year. And especially known to those, like Reagan, who had graduated from college around 1932. This is the year Foster ran for the presidency, backed by such well-known writers as Sherwood Anderson, Erskine Caldwell, Theodore Dreiser, and Upton Sinclair.

This is also like saying he was ignorant of the Bolshevik's propagandizing and recruiting of activists during the 1930s, when the depression was being depicted as "proof" of capitalism's failure and that he was unaware of their use of subversive agents both before and after U.S. recognition of the U.S.S.R. in 1933, even though a condition for recognition was to refrain from subversion. His professed naivete is especially hard to swallow since he associates it with his supposed postwar disillusionment:

> Like most of the soldiers who came back, I expected a world suddenly reformed. I hoped and believed that the . . . death and confusion of World War II would result in a regeneration of mankind. . . . If men could cooperate in war, how much better they could work together in peace!

> I was wrong. I learned that a thousand bucks under the table was the formula for buying a new car. I learned that the real estate squeeze was on for the serviceman. I discovered that the rich had got just a little richer and a lot of the poor had done a pretty good job of grabbing a quick buck. I discovered that the world was almost the same and perhaps a little worse.[75]

In no way was Reagan like "most of the soldiers who came back." First of all, he "came back" sooner than most of them, having been discharged in August 1945. Many of them, while awaiting discharge under the wartime point system, were on occupation duty in Germany or Japan. Moreover, unlike the others, he was scheduled "to work for Warner's in March of 1946." Until then, says Reagan, "I was blindly and busily joining every organization I could find that would guarantee to save the world." What he was trying to save it from is still unclear since Hitler, Mussolini, and Tojo were no longer a problem. And it couldn't have been Stalin since Reagan states, "I was not sharp about Communism: the Russians still seemed to be our allies."[76]

Reagan's talk about "coming back" and expecting "a world suddenly reformed" is contradicted by the fact that he was "stationed" in Culver City, near Hollywood, during the war. There was no reason for him to feel any different about the postwar period than anyone else in Los Angeles County, including "Rosie the riveter." Besides, as he himself admits, he was "well fixed," especially since his "$3,500-a-week contract was running."[77] Why then the disillusionment?

Equally false is Reagan's claim that "most of the soldiers who came back" were disillusioned, having "expected a world suddenly reformed." Actually most of them liked America the way it was and had no desire to change it. They were also grateful for their victory over America's enemies and thankful for still being alive, while remembering those who didn't make it. Unlike Reagan, they believed they had already "saved the world" and joined such patriotic organizations as the American Legion and Veterans of Foreign Wars. However, Reagan found these organizations "highly intolerant":

> [My] first evangelism came in the form of being
> hell-bent on saving the world from neo-Fascism.
> At that time there were visible dangers of this. I

myself observed more than forty veterans' organizations arise; most of them seemed to be highly
intolerant of color, creed, and common sense. I
joined the American Veterans Committee [AVC]
because of their feeling that the members should
be citizens first and veterans afterward [whatever
that means] . . .[78]

He doesn't explain how he knew these organizations were highly intolerant without having joined them.
Nor does he explain why he didn't know the organization he joined was a Communist front. He admits though
that, according to the California Senate Fact-Finding
Committee on Un-American Activities (1947, 1949, 1951
reports), the AVC "had become a hotbed of Communists in Hollywood."[79] Yet, why didn't he know this before the investigation since he was in this bed with them?

What Reagan liked about the AVC may be what he
also liked about the United World Federalists (renamed
the World Federalist Association, WFA) since he joined
this too, after leaving the AVC. The WFA, which is compatible with communism, is a Council on Foreign Relations (CFR) offshoot, having been founded in 1947 by
two CFR members, Norman Cousins and James P.
Warburg. Being "peace"-minded, it has much in common with the Disciples, as evident during 17-24 October
1985, in D.C., when it "hosted a 'Peace Committee' del-
egation from the Soviet Union" in return for a 1984
invitation to visit Moscow.[80]

On the day before, October 16, Reagan advocated
ratification of the Genocide Treaty.[81] This may not have
been by chance. It was also what the World Federalists
had been doing, being in accordance with their "incremental ratification approach" to world government. The
treaty, as they saw it, was another stepping stone, or
means to an end. Reagan must have known this, as the
Christian Inquirer suggests:

> With this [WFA] stepping stone plan . . . and with
> President Reagan having called for . . . ratification
> of the Genocide Treaty, it seems [possible] that
> Reagan's ideology has not changed from the 1950s
> when he was a member of the World Federalists.[82]

Under this "incremental ratification (or treaty law) approach," nations are encouraged to ratify international agreements, which eventually bring such nations under the UN's authority. Thus the WFA's goal—as one of its presidents, former Senator Joseph Clark (D-PA), disclosed—is the creation of "a universal federation of all the nation-states in a limited world government. . . ." This is why Clark wanted the UN to have, among other things, the power to tax, use of military force, and "compulsory jurisdiction over disputes between nations, whether justifiable or not, by the World Court . . . ."[83] All of this, we are to believe, would lead to "world peace." For example, at a Congressional hearing on the UN (following the WFA-Soviet "peace-in"), a WFA official, John Logue, declared: "Peace people—and all people— must see that if we really want to stop the arms race we must have effective world political institutions.

> We must stop pretending that a UN with a veto
> in its Security Council can keep the peace. . . . Yes,
> peace people must . . . tell the world's people not
> what they want to hear, but what they ought to
> hear. . . . that if we really want to stop the arms
> race, if we really want to have peace and promote
> justice, we must reform, restructure and strengthen
> the United Nations and give it the power and
> authority and funds to keep the peace and to
> promote justice . . . The [UN] must have taxing
> power . . . . It must have a large peacekeeping
> force. . . . [In] the area of peace and security, it
> must be able to make and enforce the law on the
> individual.[84]

This is the same pro-UN position that the NCC/

WCC, including the Disciples, has. For instance, at a 1980 WCC-sponsored conference in Australia, Disciples of Christ leaders "joined in recommendation that . . . the church support international bodies working for a new international economic order such as the United Nations."[85] Reagan's position is the same. In addition to promoting the Genocide Treaty, and praising the UN Declaration of Human Rights, he tried to restore Congress's 1985 cutbacks in our UN contribution (which had been slashed by about $100 million). Also, during his September 1986 UN address, he said, "My country, which has always given the UN generous support, will continue to play a leading role in the effort to achieve its noble purposes."[86]

The WFA, NCC/WCC, and the UN are all part of the "world solidarity revolution"—along with the many other organizations associated with "liberal" Protestantism, "Catholic" modernism, Illuminism, Freemasonry, New Ageism, secular humanism, the "liberal" Eastern Establishment, and international communism (including Fabian socialism). As for the World Council of Churches, a Club of Rome report (*Goals for Mankind*) says:

> with its 285 member churches in all parts of the world, [it] examines issues of global relevance, and has come out with recommendations for creating a just and sustainable world society. It has set itself the task of encouraging the promotion of world peace with justice and freedom . . . .
>
> The similar humanitarian world concerns of the Roman Catholic Church [i.e., its left-wing faction], and the individual initiatives of particular Christian Churches, are moving Christians everywhere toward global consciousness and world solidarity.[87]

A "world society," "world peace," "global consciousness," and "world solidarity" are also what the Communists want. This is why communism is part of the "world solidarity revolution," which includes the "revolution of rising expectations."[88] Even the Club of Rome says so: "Marxist humanism . . . throws a distinctive light on the issue of contemporary world solidarity."[89] As for "world peace": "[The] struggle for communism . . . is intrinsically bound up with the struggle for peace in the world."[90] This is why, as defense official Marian Leighton explains, the Soviets "[play] upon the WCC's internationalist spirit and its desire to unify the Christian churches, end social injustice around the globe, and promote disarmament, [thus engaging it] in their worldwide 'united front' strategy against the Western democracies. This strategy makes use of non-Communist groups—from Social Democratic parties to labor unions to Christian and Islamic bodies—to spread Soviet influence under the slogan of a 'struggle for peace' "[91]

No WCC denomination struggles harder "for peace" than the Disciples. Though frequently using the words "unity," "justice," and "disarmament," nothing turns them on more than "peace." Thus the dove is their favorite symbol, which possibly even upstages the cross. Their obsession with it, or what it signifies, is noticeable in their official publication, *The Disciple*. An example is their January 1986 edition wherein ten of the twelve items in the News Briefs section concern "peace": a peace library, a shalom candle, a peace question, a shalom committee, action for peace and justice, a film festival called "Peace A La Mode," a dove representing peace, a shalom congregation, a peace education event, and "peace-pairing" of U.S. and Soviet cities. Also, one of the two adjacent ads has a dove in it.[92]

The Disciples use the word "peace" with almost everything, especially in regard to disarmament, the defense industry, nuclear energy, and human rights. Even their prayers are padded with it. Some Disciples churches are little more than centers of left-wing political activity, rather than worship. Through their Shalom Congregation Program, which involves "consciousness-raising," entire congregations are indoctrinated in the various "peace"-related issues, using prayers, sermons, Sunday school, evening studies, fellowship dinners, political role-playing activities, training programs in civil disobedience, political letter-writing, "peace" protests, and trips to Communist countries. However, unwary visitors may not even notice the program since its activities, having a religious facade, are usually presented as being divinely inspired. A Disciples minister describes his program: "A short worship service is part of each task force meeting, serving to remind us that the . . . foundation of shalom is in our relationship with God. . . .

> Shalom was the topic of one of a series of church-wide human interest mini-courses. U.S. Representative Tom Harkin spoke on "Human Rights Issues in Central America." . . . A telephone network was established among members of the church to inform them of issues coming before the congress and the state legislature. A "Shalom Corner" has been included in each issue of The Link, our weekly newsletter.

> Sermons, scriptures [sic] and pastoral prayers often include the theme of shalom. The elders include some concept of shalom in their communion prayers. The congregation is greeted with "shalom" during the welcome time and the benediction always ends with the phrase, "People of God, go in shalom." A large shalom banner hangs at the front of the sanctuary and a "Shalom Thought" is included in the worship bulletin each Sunday.[93]

Reagan also, in a sense, had a Shalom program—in the White House, as evident before, during, and even after the Geneva summit. Before it began, for example, he called himself "a husband, father, and grandfather who shares your deepest hopes that all our children can live and prosper in a world of peace." Also: (1) "Americans are a peace-loving people"; (2) "We seek peace not only for ourselves but for all those who inhabit this small planet"; (3) "Let us hope that as we near Christmas and the New Year that this will be a season for peace."

By the time it began, even the Soviets were sick of the word, as when Tass snipped: "Really . . . the head of the administration uttered a good many words about peace . . . but . . ."[94]

Yet, Reagan's shalomming continued, throughout the summit and even afterward, saying that "[while others had failed to achieve] a more stable and peaceful relationship with the Soviet Union, [he would] build a foundation for lasting peace." Adding: "[True] peace rests on the pillars of individual freedom, human rights . . . and respect for the rule of law." Concerning people-to-people exchanges, he gushed: "[They will] build in our societies thousands of coalitions for cooperation and peace," as well as "genuine constituencies for peace in both countries." Why was he there? "My mission, simply stated, is a mission for peace." Then he cooed: "We understand each other better. That's the key to peace. . . . We know that peace is not just the absence of war. We don't want a phony peace or a frail peace. . . . We want real peace."[95] Finally: "Let us hope that these words will be the foundation for making 1986 the year of peace our peoples deserve."[96]

THREE

And More Peace

A study of the Disciples' Shalom program, during Reagan's first term, reveals that many of its activists were church officials, school administrators, politicians, and even federal employees. It is therefore significant that the program included nuclear disarmament protests, sheltering of Central American refugees, and workshops on U.S.-U.S.S.R. relations and the SDI. What especially made this program influential was its inclusion of other denominations such as Lutherans, Presbyterians, United Methodists, and the United Church of Christ. As *The Disciple* described it, the program "focuses on involving entire communities of faith in study and work for a safer, more equitable world."[1]

However, because of their quest for church unity, the Disciples also saw the program as a means for achieving such unity. That is, it enabled them to form partnerships with other denominations through mutual involvement in "peace"-related activities. This was better than just talking, which usually resulted in little, if any, action. An exception was when the United Church of Christ (which is historically related to the Disciples) agreed to form an "ecumenical partnership" with them. This meant they would be jointly involved in such issues as "peace with justice, education, recruitment and placement of racial/ethnic clergy, building local congregations, and economic justice and human equality."[2]

The Isaacs (*The Coercive Utopians*) mention that United Church of Christ officials "are among the most prominent radical activists." An example is Reverend Ben Chavis who was "one of the Wilmington 10 accused of firebombing a grocery store in North Carolina." He also, in 1978, compiled the infamous list of so-called political prisoners in the U.S., which included Puerto Rican terrorists. This list was used by the United Church of Christ to support the false allegations made by UN Ambassador Andrew Young (CFR), another United Church of Christ minister.

While in jail, Chavis served with the United Church of Christ's Commission for Racial Justice, receiving about $425,000 of the denomination's tithes for the Wilmington Ten's defense. Though he wasn't convicted, Chavis remained contemptuous of our society, eventually becoming co-chairman (along with Angela Davis, a U.S. Communist Party leader) of the National Alliance Against Racist and Political Repression. "[At] the February 1980 rally against the Klan at Greensboro, North Carolina, Chavis vowed that there would be no draft: 'If we're going to fight, we're going to fight right here in the U.S.' And Chavis shouted: 'We're going to march; we're going to keep on marching until we tear this system down.' "[3]

In November 1983, Chavis showed up at Reagan's alma mater, Eureka College, as an honored guest. In fact, he delivered the prestigious 1983 Humbert Lecture on the 8th. His speech, entitled "The Theology and Politics of 1984," was intellectually dull, a regurgitation of the same old leftist clichés associated with liberation theology. Evoking guilt, he claimed the only real threat to world peace was the U.S., reminding the audience that "only one nation in the world had dropped [an atomic] bomb on human beings, and that was [ours]." He also said we have a responsibility "to defend the poor" and "seek world order and justice." Then, questioning our spirit of nationalism, he remarked: "I don't think we have any right to use our military forces to dominate anyone else. The history of our country has shown that our military has been used not in the interest of liberation, but domination."[4]

Chavis was rewarded with a loud, hearty applause. None of his allegations concerning the U.S. were rebutted, nor were the Communist atrocities in Afghanistan, Cambodia, South Africa, or anywhere else, mentioned. Even the Soviets' September attack on KAL Flight 007, with 269 innocent people aboard, was ignored. Instead, Chavis was seen as a contemporary hero for Eureka's students to emulate.

Chavis's warm welcome was in sharp contrast to the school administration's cold cancellation of Jerry Falwell's 7 October 1985 visit, which the Young Republicans had arranged. The reason given was that it would conflict with the 5 October inauguration of the school's new president, George Hearne, a Disciples minister. Besides, they said, 5 October was during the homecoming weekend. None of this, of course, was a problem several months earlier when Falwell's visit was planned.[5]

Later, articles about Chavis appeared in the school's two major publications: one in its newspaper, *The Pegasus* (28 November 1983), and another in its quarterly, *News and Ideas* (December 1983). Even his photograph, along with a smaller one of Reagan, was placed in the school's 1984-85 catalog.

In *The Pegasus'* same edition is an article about an evening "vesper service," called "Dare to Oppose Worship of a Nation-State," to be held in the chapel on 29 November. However, a copy of the program reveals that the "service" was actually a "peace" indoctrination, as seen in its "Prayer for Peace" (to be read in unison):

> God of peace and love, whom thy people crucify anew whenever they rebuild the golden calf of national idolatry in war: we need to be reminded, that they who love the greater love give of their life, but do not hate or justify themselves in self-congratulation . . . Grant us courage, in this age which teeters on the edge of nuclear holocaust, to seek boldly for leadership and self-dedication in our social and political life, which will build a way

safe for our children . . . We call upon you . . . in
the spirit of the Prince of Peace. Amen.

This was followed by a reading during a period of
meditation:

> Consider quietly that . . . God's purpose might be
> to save mankind from the unthinkable possibility
> it has created for itself—an atomic holocaust.
> There are now more bombs on both sides than
> there are targets! It is doubtful whether once
> begun, a nuclear conflict could ever be controlled.
> Its beginning then, represents the ending of life
> itself. . . . Do the bomb makers (G.E. and others)
> want to return all existence to the time before the
> creation—literal nothingness, as the fate of the
> planet Earth?[6]

The program lists Glenn Riddell (college chaplain)
as the liturgist and a reader, and Royal Humbert (professor emeritus) as the interpreter. Also listed are organizations associated with "arms control and refugee issues" such as:

> A.D.A. Political Action Committee
> American Civil Liberties Union
> Center for Defense Information
> Clergy and Laity Concerned
> Common Cause
> Disciples Peace Fellowship
> Physicians for Social Responsibility
> Sane
> Union of Concerned Scientists
> Amnesty International
> Council for a Livable World.

Eureka's chapel, especially McCallister Hall
(wherein this "service" was held), is used for worship,
concerts, lectures, and other cultural events. Completed
in 1869, it is listed in the National Register of Historic
Places. It is also a place that Reagan and his brother, as
students, often visited.

On 13 December, about two weeks later, the faculty-trustee dinner was held at the Peoria Country Club. The dining room was festively decorated for the holiday season and, recalls a faculty member, peppermint ice cream was served. Though delicious, it was painful to eat because of the ground-up candy canes in it. Also painful was the awareness of a student having committed suicide in his dorm earlier that evening. While talk about it was tactfully avoided, much of the conversation concerned Reagan possibly visiting the school in February.

The exact date was still unknown and remained so until mid-January. It was then announced that Reagan would speak on 6 February, his 73rd birthday. His speech would serve two purposes: (1) as the Founders Day address to commemorate the school's 129th birthday; (2) to begin *Time* magazine's new Distinguished Speakers Program. The affair, as planned, was to be a formal assembly, including a faculty procession in academic robes and regalia. But, in the interest of "peace," this plan was soon scrapped—dumped on the altar of Shalom.

That is, on 19 January, certain faculty/staff members devised a letter of protest questioning the moral basis for Reagan's foreign policy and fictitious "strategic arms buildup." This letter was *selectively* circulated and given to the local *Woodford County Journal* for publication. It says the protesters plan to wear "white arm bands [with doves on them]" during Reagan's speech and hold public "prayer meetings . . . before and after."[7] Also, it states: "[Many] feel that we are closer to a global nuclear war than [ever before] . . . because of [Reagan's] arms build-up and . . . intervention in Central America, the Caribbean, and the Middle East." It continues:

> Currently, we face a 200 billion dollar deficit, but while most areas of the budget have been trimmed, defense expenditures climb. . . .

The U.S. Catholic bishops have issued a strong statement on behalf of moral strength and against the current arms build-up. In their view, [this] build-up is immoral because it a) [sic] robs funds desperately needed by the poor in this and other countries for food . . . b) [sic] produces weapons which have no value other than [for deterrence]. . . . [The missiles] would severely disrupt the world's ecosystems, resulting in mass extinction of many species, a year-long nuclear winter, [and] the certain death of almost all human [beings].[8]

Though most of the non-protesters were faint-hearted, the more principled ones were openly critical of the letter. A few were even confrontational, which included hassling with the school president, "Dr." Gilbert. They argued that wearing arm bands would cheapen the occasion. It would also be intimidating and disruptive, possibly creating divisions within the faculty. Besides, they asked, what right do the protesters have to determine school policy? But, like the alcohol problem, Gilbert sought a political "solution." He simply cancelled the faculty procession and wearing of academic robes. The arm bands were okay though.

On 6 February, while waiting in the gym for Reagan to show, the protesters were standing in order to flaunt their arm bands with the doves on them. They seemed boorish since almost everyone else was seated. Earlier they had been demonstrating outside the gym, called Reagan Center; but, being an extremely cold day, their zeal had waned with the temperature of their feet. They had also been snubbed by the passersby, while to the reporters (who were inside getting warm) they were nonexistent. Nothing worked. They would have been better off in their robes.

Reagan undoubtedly knew about the protest when it first started. His brother Neil, a Eureka trustee, would have told him about it. He was scheduled to visit the school, too. Gilbert, also, would have told him. Yet, Reagan himself usually kept an eye on the place, in various ways—and for various reasons. He even knew about the suicide, since he sent the victim's parents "a condolence letter."[9]

When Reagan appeared on the stage, everyone immediately responded with a standing ovation, followed by the "happy birthday song." Next to him were Nancy, Neil, and Gilbert. Also present were James Thompson, governor of Illinois, and Henry Grunwald (CFR), *Time* magazine's editor-in-chief. Special guests in the audience were Hasib Sabbagh and his daughter Sana, who had just graduated from Harvard. Sabbagh, chairman of Consolidated Contractors International (Athens, Greece), had earlier pledged $500 thousand to the Reagan scholarship program, which was in addition to the $100 thousand given in 1983. According to *News and Ideas,*

> Sabbagh has a particular interest in international education. He has indicated a continuing concern for assisting Eureka College and the Reagan Scholarships to develop a more sophisticated international perspective among American college graduates.[10]

Reagan's speech, besides being a web of lies, was ambiguous. It was also pacifistic: "We've tried to bring a new honesty and moral purposefulness to our foreign policy, to show we can be candid about the essential differences between ourselves and others while still pursuing peace initiatives with them." Some other gems were: (1) "We're trying to see to it that American citizens . . . can no longer be attacked or their lives endangered with impunity"; (2) "[The] excitement and energy in the intellectual world is focused these days on the concerns of human freedom, on the importance of transcendent and enduring values"; (3) "[We] are returning now to . . . limited government, the defense of freedom, faith in the future and in our God"; (4) "[The future holds] out not only the promise of sweeping improvements in mankind's material conditions but progress in the spiritual and moral realm as well."[11] He "also called for arms reduction in light of an inadequate arms control policy."[12] Finally, he sighed: "May God bless this campus 'neath the elms."

Thus the protesters were criticizing someone like themselves. Why? The Reagan delusion. Having been deluded, they were now deluding others—like the media, depicting him as a conservative, anti-Communist Republican. But that's not all. They were Shalomniks, bored and in need of self-expression. That is, they were little people at a little college in a little town with little to see and little to do. They needed to protest—and they needed this event. Since it drew about 2000 locals, and had nationwide coverage, it was an irresistible opportunity.

On the following day, faculty members found little pink notices in their mail boxes. They were actually invitations to attend an "open-forum" called "What's The Dove All About?" This meeting (moderated by the dean of the faculty, whose wife was the Christian Church's secretary) "[concerned the] question that the armbands raised." The notice said: "[The] visity [sic] this past weekend by President Reagon [sic] brought mixed feelings to the Eureka College community." It added,

> One group [responded] to a certain feeling and belief they had about the issue of peace by wearing armbands with doves on them. This, however, caused some bad feelings. . . .

> [Tomorrow there] will be . . . an open-forum concerning . . . the armbands. . . . We will have representatives from both sides of the issue invited to share their feelings. This is not intended as a debate but merely . . . a chance to hear how others feel.

Contact Chaplain Riddell if you . . . would like to express your feelings.[13]

This emphasis on "feelings" suggested it would be more like group therapy, which would be pointless since everyone's "feelings" were already known. Thus few, if any, of the non-protesters showed up. Besides, as they knew, it could only serve the interests of "the doves," which they were called by then.

Meanwhile a group of Disciples churches, called the Illinois Valley Cluster, were trying to acquire a radio station. One of them was the Eureka Christian Church. Reagan's alma mater was also involved. They had formed the Illinois Valley Broadcasting Corporation (IVBC) and were holding monthly meetings at the First (American) Baptist Church in Peoria. The IVBC's purpose was to: (1) "provide an ecumenical Christian Radio Broadcasting voice in Central Illinois representing the mainline churches"; (2) "offer an alternative style and choice in religious programs."[14] Besides Disciples, certain other denominations were also represented on its board of directors. They were:

United Church of Christ
Presbyterian Church (USA)
American Baptist Church
Reformed Church in America
Church of the Brethren
Lutheran Church in America
United Methodist Church

On 23 January, just before Reagan's visit, the board met to discuss the IVBC's brochure and programming policy, among other things. The brochure, which was being revised, implied that Christian fundamentalism was a problem and so something had to be done about it. It warned:

Radio and TV airways are dominated by individuals and churches basically representing a funda-

> mentalist viewpoint which is . . . a partisan per-
> spective.
>
> There are at present some 1400 radio ministries
> in this country and . . . there are about 14 million
> people who are being influenced by these minis-
> tries.[15]

Thus, to liberate this captive audience from its oppressors, the IVBC planned to "offer an alternative style and choice in religious programs." There would be, for instance, "local talk shows presenting a balanced perspective which challenges the person of faith." There would also be: (1) "Bible study [under] prominent Biblical scholars"; (2) "Religious music representing a wide range of styles"; (3) "Review of current events from the perspective of a Christian." Of course, by "perspective of a Christian," the IVBC meant its own perspective, which was that of the National/World Council of Churches.[16]

Missing from IVBC's programming policy (second draft) is the word "Bible." This, presumably, is because IVBC's "intent [was] to stimulate the minds and spirits of our listeners so that they will want to explore the writings, teachings, and ideas of the great scholars, philosophers, and theologians." However, one may ask, what's wrong with exploring the Bible? As the fundamentalists do? Why is it necessary "to explore the . . . ideas of the great scholars [and] philosophers"? What would this have to do with Christianity? Such exploration might even entail an uncritical discussion of the various isms, including mysticism and occultism, even more so since, according to its Statement of Principles, the "IVBC intends always to be [politically] impartial—recognizing that people of good conscience are found on both sides of most every political question, and that easy answers are seldom truly satisfactory, and that freedom and peace and justice are the heartfelt goals of virtually everyone."

Another IVBC principle was "[to be] ecumenical." That is, "to unite Christians of all denominations and, under a Christian format, to extend understanding to all faiths." But this would be a rejection of the essential, or fundamental doctrines of the Christian faith. One other was "[to be] seeking." By this, they meant "[to seek] God's guidance," which, of course, one should do. However, what they also meant, digressively, was: "Expressing Christian principals [sic] of morality in a way that builds on the best of human achievement and works toward the goal of establishing God's kingdom on earth." This, though, is unscriptural. It is also inconceivable; for in no way could God's kingdom be established by man alone, especially through the apostate World Council of Churches.

The Illinois Valley Cluster, wherein the IVBC originated, was under the influence of the Disciples' Shalom Congregation Program. This program, as said earlier, is associated with the Riverside Church in New York. However, the main source of the Riverside disarmament program's speakers and publications is the Institute for Policy Studies (IPS), a radical pro-Soviet think tank.[17]

The IPS' connection with the KGB is well-known, having been instrumental in the Soviets' dissemination of propaganda and misintelligence. Such misinformation, which hurt America's image, helped the Soviets to achieve their foreign policy goals. This IPS-KGB conduit also enabled them to obtain names of individuals who could be used as dupes or even Soviet agents, called "secret assets." Louise Rees, a former House Internal Security Committee researcher, explains:

> In matters involving the covert insertion of a Soviet voice into the public debate in the United States, the International Department [of the Central Committee] calls on K.G.B. intelligence officers and secret "assets" they have cultivated in the U.S. media, academia, government, and other

circles which affect public opinion and U.S. policy. These subversive operations, "active measures" to the K.G.B., constitute the "unconventional political warfare" component to the Kremlin's overt foreign-policy initiatives.[18]

IPS even set up a joint disarmament program with the U.S.S.R.-U.S.A. Friendship Society and the Soviets' Institute for the U.S.A. and Canada (IUSAC). The purpose of this program (largely under KGB supervision) was to give the impression that America was to blame for the arms race.[19] Such manipulation of public opinion was crucial to Soviet foreign policy, which dovetailed with our own (i.e., Rocky-Bye-Baby's)—paving the way for world government. In collusion with these entities (in the name of "world peace") is the World Council of Churches. Marian Leighton notes:

> The Rev. William Sloane Coffin, whose Riverside Church in New York hosted a WCC-sponsored Program to Combat Racism, with the participation of pro-Communist and Soviet-front groups, has exclaimed that "[Americans] and the Soviets, if not one in love, are one in sin." Ascribing such moral equivalence to the two superpowers is a deliberate disinformation effort designed to make Soviet policies more acceptable to democratic societies.[20]

Most of IPS' funds came from the Samuel Rubin Foundation. Other sources were: the Marshall Field Foundation, Janss Foundation, and the Joint Foundation Support Corporation (consisting of nine foundations). Some of IPS' numerous offshoots received grants from, among others, the Rockefeller Brothers Foundation, Ford Foundation, and Reagan's Department of Energy.[21]

Rubin, prior to World War II, had registered in elections as a Communist party member. Following his death, his daughter, Cora Weiss, became the foundation's vice-president. She also directed the Riverside Church Disarmament Program, which may explain the IPS-Riverside connection.[22] Rees reveals: "Mrs. Weiss and her husband, National Lawyers Guild member Peter Weiss, play a leading role in financing the Institute for Policy Studies in Washington, which has established cooperative arrangements with several Moscow-based organizations involved in 'active measures.' "[23]

One of IPS' most important offshoots is the Center for Defense Information (CDI), which was listed in Eureka's Vesper Service program. Both organizations were noted for downplaying the Soviet threat, opposing key U.S. military projects, and disseminating false defense-related information. CDI's appearance of having credibility was largely due to: (1) its official-like name; (2) its director, Gene R. LaRocque, being a retired Navy admiral. As to CDI's sophistry, the Isaacs state:

> The [Soviets'] actions . . . even . . . the invasion of Afghanistan, are portrayed as defensive in intent. According to [CDI], the Soviets only invaded Afghanistan because they believed the United States had repudiated detente. [LaRocque says] the Cubans are in Africa because "they have an affinity to the people they see who appear to be downtrodden and who need help." On a trip to Cuba at the invitation of Castro in June 1980, LaRocque concluded that the Soviet impact there was minimal . . . that "Soviet influence on Cuba's military, from what I could see, was almost non-existent." The Center explains our unreasonable fear of the Soviet Union as "emotional."[24]

Even LaRocque showed up at Reagan's alma mater . . . naturally. He was a panel member at the 5-8 June 1984 conference called "Peace with Justice," which was funded by "a $27,080 grant from the Disciples Division of Higher Education." With him were: (1) former Defense undersecretary Fred Ikle; (2) Mexican Nobel

Prize winner (world peace) Garcia Robles; (3) Goshen Biblical Seminary professor John Howard Yoder. Yoder (the conference's theologian-in-residence) led the "participants in a consideration of how the gospel and Christian faith [reflected] on the information provided." As *The Disciple* reported: "The panelists are the experts, but even the experts disagree," says Glenn Riddell, chaplain of Eureka College and director of the conference. "We hope to present all sides so that all participants can make their own determination based on accurate information, informed opinion and the inspiration of their own faith."[25]

To "present all sides" would have been impossible since all of the panelists were on the same side. While Ikle was a former Disarmament Agency director, Robles's Nobel Prize was for "his work on disarmament." Ikle, a Council on Foreign Relations member, was succeeded by another CFR member, Paul Warnke, also a Trilateralist. Although Ikle knew about State Department Publication 7277 (*Freedom From War*) and the related Phoenix Papers, these treacherous documents were ignored. Even though "7277" is still in effect. Author James D. Bales (*The Phoenix Papers: If Not Treason, What?*) writes: "[The] fundamental assumption [found in these papers] is that, given enough time, cooperative association with Communists will change both of us, so that we shall more-or-less converge rather than have a . . . war."[26] As for LaRocque:

> [In 1975, he] used his credibility as a former admiral to produce a crisis . . . with Japan, telling a [congressional] subcommittee that the [U.S.] did not honor agreements to off-load atomic weapons from U.S. warships before they entered Japanese harbors. [He] then went to Moscow as a guest of the [IUSAC]. . . . There LaRocque, after having produced [a] furor in Japan, admitted to . . . the Japanese Communist Party newspaper *Akahata* that "he had never called at a Japanese

port aboard a U.S. ship which was . . . carrying nuclear weaponry."[27]

There seemed to be no end to the pacifistic activities at Eureka, such as the 23 January 1985 lecture on the "Just War Theory"; the 30 January 1985 slide presentation on a Eureka trustee's 11-day tour of the Soviet Union (sponsored by the National Council of Churches); and the 17-18 April 1985 anti-apartheid presentations by two groups: the American Friends Service Committee (AFSC) and the Coalition for Illinois Divestment from South Africa (CIDSA).

The AFSC's key speaker was Tandi Gcabasche, exiled daughter of Nobel Prize recipient (world peace) Albert Lithuli. Her views coincided with those of the African National Congress (ANC). Her discourse took the form of emotionally-loaded misinformation designed to confuse and anger. She even associated apartheid with Nazism: "The homelands to me are just like concentration camps—only the Nazis used gas chambers while South Africa lets us starve to death."[28] The ANC's burning them "to death" was okay though, since it wasn't mentioned.

On the following day, she spoke again, but with the CIDSA. This group's regular speakers were David Mesenbring, a Luthern World Ministries official, and Orlando Redekopp, an integrated Chicago church minister. Redekopp called apartheid "a system of slavery," adding: U.S. corporations exploit this "slave labor." Later, Gcabasche said: "As U.S. investments have increased . . . conditions for . . . blacks have become worse." She also expressed agreement with Bishop Tutu that, "We don't want our chains polished, we want them removed!"[29]

While most of the audience was taken in by this slavery pitch, at least one person wasn't: Reverend Gary M. Hedrick, a Bob Jones University graduate. Hedrick was also the local Liberty Bible Church's pastor. His church—unlike the Disciples' large, permanent structure—was what used to be a furniture store, complete with a wide, plate-glass front. In a letter to Eureka's chaplain, he wrote:

> My objection to the presentation . . . was not that they were allowed to present their views, but that the presentation was one-sided . . . To present only one side of such a vital and far-reaching issue, it seems to me, is irresponsible . . . especially for a college which is supposed to be committed to academic freedom and the presentation of a wide range of perspectives on issues. As a conservative Christian, it bothers me to see only a leftist/liberal perspective consistently presented in many of our so-called "Christian" academic institutions.
>
> . . . Mr. Grobler [S.A. Consulate General] told me on the phone that he would have been happy to have been present for the seminar on April 18, but he was not invited. This makes me wonder if there was some reason why Eureka College wanted only one side of this issue presented. Perhaps I have an overly active imagination.[30]

Actually, Hedrick's imagination wasn't "overly active" at all. He knew Reagan's alma mater, a Disciples institution, was pushing the NCC/WCC's pro-ANC agenda. He also knew the ANC was controlled by the South African Communist Party (SACP), which was controlled by the Soviets. Who, in a sense, were controlled by Rocky-Bye. As Igor Glagolev, a former Soviet official (African Affairs), disclosed, "The Soviet leadership controls not only the South African Communist party but the African National Congress."[31]

FOUR

Blood, Bones, and the Kingdom of God

The Christian Church (Disciples of Christ) itself compares apartheid to Nazism. This evokes Auschwitz-like images of barbed wire, gas chambers, and furnaces, as though South Africa had its own "final solution." Even the Disciples' president, John O. Humbert, made this analogy: "The South African government has made racial oppression a part of Christian doctrine, just as Hitler did."[1]

He says the "established German Protestants were accepting the Hitler doctrine that Jews were an inferior race and that the role of the church was to support the German government unquestioningly." As to the anti-Nazi Christians (who issued the Barmen Declaration): "But the faithful few in the Confessing Church countered that it is the Christian's duty to obey God, not humans, which they also supported with scripture. Many of [them] would pay with their lives. . . ." He then mentions that their "Barmen Declaration was recalled a few months ago as church leaders from ten western countries met in Harare, Zimbabwe, with church leaders from South Africa, including Nobel Prize winner [world peace] Bishop Desmond Tutu."

Humbert is referring to the special WCC meeting held 4-6 December 1985, which led to the Harare Declaration, urging the overthrow of South Africa by way of economic sanctions, civil disobedience, labor unrest, and "the immediate implementation of [UN] Resolution 435 on Namibia." It also called "on the church inside and outside South Africa to support SA movements working for the liberation of their country."[2] Then, reinforcing the South Africa-Nazi Germany analogy, Humbert quotes Tutu: "The Harare Declaration is as important to our struggle as the Barmen Declaration was to the confessing churches in Germany."[3]

Humbert and Tutu ignore the fact that of over 100 participants in the Harare conference, about half of them were uninvited radicals who manipulated the meetings. Moreover, notes Siegfried Ernst, former president of the Synod of Württemberg, Germany, "Nothing was put to the vote—resolutions were only formulated. Such is the racist-socialist understanding of democracy in the church."[4]

Humbert also overlooks the fact that the Harare Declaration can be traced to the 13 September 1985 Marxist-Leninist Kairos Document. According to *Signposts,* a South African periodical, this document "clearly rejects the traditional, Biblical understanding of Christianity and replaces it with the fundamental principles of Marxism!" Also: "[Because] it knows that Christians would reject Marxism if it were presented as such, it makes Marxism acceptable to them as a new interpretation of Christianity!"[5] But there is more. Prior to Harare, South Africa's Gospel Defence League warned:

> [The] Kairos Document is an open call to rebellion, revolution, violence and possibly assassination. . . . [It] is a treasonable paper, and [it is not surprising] that its author(s) prefer(s) to remain anonymous. It is a massive onslaught against biblical Christianity and God's law order, and both Church and State should view it in an extremely serious light. . . .

> . . . [The] Kairos "theologians" call for world support of their plans. They will no doubt receive it in full measure at the "Emergency Meeting of the World Council of Churches" in Harare from 4-6 December 85, and world pressure on South Africa will . . . increase once again as a result.[6]

This is precisely what happened. Also, as *Signposts* said, Marxism was made acceptable to the gullible through reinterpretation of Scripture. Thus, through inversion, Christians who supported South Africa's Marxist-Leninist revolutionaries were equated with Christians who opposed the Nazis. This, figuratively, implies that the ANC terrorists would have been champions of the Jews and that, since God is on their side, their "necklacing" of politically incorrect blacks was divinely inspired.

Actually, the World Council of Churches is more like the pro-Nazi German church. The Nazis, like the WCC-backed Marxist-Leninist states, were also socialistic (nationally), deterministic (racially), anti-capitalistic, anti-Semitic, and terroristic. While the Nazis' "revolutionary principle" was race rather than class, they were as far left on the political spectrum as the Marxist-Leninist Socialists (i.e., Communists) since both require a totalitarian, Orwellian-like polity. (On the far right then, contrary to lib-prop, are the anarchists who desire the absence of political authority.) Hitler himself was a Socialist, and, writes Paul Johnson (*Modern Times*): "Like Lenin and Stalin, Hitler believed in ultimate social engineering. The notion of destroying huge categories of people whose existence imperilled his historic mission was to him, as to them, entirely acceptable."[7]

The Disciples' identification with the anti-Nazi church gives the false impression of their being for truth and justice. Humbert says Christians should realize "that Jesus publicly announced his mission . . . as to set at liberty those who are oppressed." Then, without compassion for the ANC's victims (many of whom were Christians), he adds: "[Jesus strongly criticized] religious people who . . . neglected the 'really important things' like justice and mercy." As in liberation theology, the Disciples often use Scripture arbitrarily to support whatever they do. Thus, playing "God's children," they can deem anything they oppose as being evil. Humbert, for example, remarked: "[The Barmen Declaration] was re-called again [after Harare] when 125 persons from twenty-five Protestant, Orthodox and Roman Catholic churches met at the Disciples National City Christian Church in Washington, D.C., to establish an emergency action committee [for ending] the South Africa racial separation policy called 'apartheid.' " He then describes this meeting:

> Apartheid is an "unmitigated evil, the product of sin and the work of the devil," said the National City gathering. "Economic pressure on South Africa is the most important non-violent method for helping to end the apartheid system."

> The time is very, very late, my friends. The South Africa situation is plunging relentlessly toward a horrible bloodbath. . . . A deputy U.S. Secretary of State once said the Bible is the most revolutionary book available in the third world. It underscores the equal worth of every human being and the promise of abundant life. . . .

> We might remember our own Boston Massacre in which five persons—including a black—died in protest of British oppression as we remember those hundreds killed in Soweto a decade ago, June 16.[8]

Humbert's reference to the Boston Massacre is inappropriate. It is also spurious. This so-called massacre was an isolated incident, beginning when some men and boys, though unprovoked, threw snowballs and rocks at a squad of British soldiers. It had nothing to do with "British oppression," as Humbert put it. All but two of the soldiers were later acquitted by a colonial jury. The lawyer who defended the officer-in-charge, Captain Preston, was one of the revolution's leaders: John Adams, our second president.[9]

While the Disciples define apartheid as an "unmitigated evil," they see nothing evil in using terrorism to change such policy. They apparently believe that God would sanction the bludgeoning, dismemberment, and burning alive of innocent people, as their pro-ANC position implies. Commenting on apartheid, *The Disciple's* editor (James L. Merrell) writes:

> One thing is clear. There can be no more gradualism or token tinkering with apartheid. The whole system must be dismantled because it is evil. Bishop Tutu says that "if someone were to show me that the Bible supports apartheid, I would burn my Bible and stop being a Christian." Christians have no option but to oppose any system that in its basic philosophy and structure denies the gospel.[10]

The Disciples have a deep feeling of reverence for Tutu, who was enthroned as the new Anglican Archbishop of Cape Town on 7 September 1986. This profound awe for him is evident in *The Disciple's* June 1986 edition wherein he appears in a full-page spread. Shown in prayer, of course, he is referred to as "that diminutive giant who is one of God's great gifts to our age . . ."[11] Even though (on 23 November 1978 in Pretoria's St. Alban's Cathedral) he preached: "The Holy Spirit is not limited to the Christian Church. For example, Mahatma Gandhi, who is a Hindu . . . The Holy Spirit shines through him."[12]

A few years later, he said, "Some people thought there was something odd about Jesus' birth . . . It may be that Jesus was an illegitimate son." Some other bits-o-wisdom were: (1) "Thank God I'm black. White people will have a lot to answer for at the last judgement"; (2) "Every Christian must be a revolutionary. Jesus was a revolutionary. I am a revolutionary . . ."; (3) "[Nelson] Mandela is my leader"; (4) "I am a socialist"; (5) "When justice prevails over injustice as in [Marxist] Zimbabwe, it shows that the kingdom of God is here already."[13]

This association of Communism with the kingdom

of God is often made by liberation theologians such as Tutu. Another one is Ernesto Cardenal, the Nicaraguan Catholic priest. Cardenal, "a self-avowed Communist," said that a "world of perfect Communism is the kingdom of God on earth. They are the same thing for me." He also said: (1) "Let us not forget that the first Christians were the best Christians, i.e., revolutionary and subversive Christians"; (2) "Marxism is the fruit of Christianity; without Christianity, Marxism would be impossible"; (3) "I believe that the Communists, too, belong to the church. I believe the true church includes many who don't perceive themselves as Christians, even those who consider themselves atheists"; (4) "For me the God of the Bible is also the God of Marxism-Leninism."[14]

Such thinking has its origin in the "social gospel" and is seen in the writings of such twentieth-century Socialist theologians as Walter Rauschenbusch, Washington Gladden, G. Bromley Oxnam, John C. Bennett, Reinhold Niebuhr, and Harry F. Ward. All of whom, not coincidentally, were associated with the Federal Council of Churches (FCC), called the National Council of Churches (NCC) after 1950. (It was the NCC from which, in 1948, the WCC evolved.[15]) Thus the FCC's Statement and Resolution (presented during the FCC's first meeting in 1908) was influenced by the writings of Rauschenbusch, Gladden, and Ward.[16] As for Rauschenbusch and Ward, Gary Allen writes:

> Rauschenbusch, an avowed socialist, knew that his teachings would be rejected by the majority if they were understood. Therefore, he took it upon himself to give new meanings to already existing Christian terms. . . .

> For example, according to Rauschenbusch's "new" theology, "sin" described the injustices that can result from private ownership of property; "salvation" referred to the public ownership of all means of production; and "the kingdom of God" was the

term meant for the established earthly Utopia as dreamed by the One Worlders. . . .

. . . Also dedicated to the world government concept was Dr. Harry F. Ward [who was identified as a Communist]. . . .

What, then, is the chief purpose of the . . . churches which have become dominated by the One World thrust of [the NCC/ WCC]? Following the dictates of the New World Order, many church leaders are as zealous as missionaries in their effort to replace the free nations of the world with a system of world government.[17]

More precisely, these "church leaders" belong to the solidarity revolution's advance guard, being "zealous . . . in their effort" to raise the level of global consciousness.[18] Knowing that a "new world order will come about . . . when a new global ethos emerges based on trust and solidarity; when a new standard of humanism crystallizes as the norm . . . ."[19] That is, they are revolutionaries with a revolutionary cause, "the kingdom of God," while being governed by a revolutionary conscience (i.e., that which advances their cause is justified). This is why they support terrorism with tithings and admire people like Cardenal and Tutu whose views are blasphemous and hostile. Two examples of Tutu's racial hatred are: (1) "Imagine what would happen if only 30 percent of domestic servants (in white households) would poison their employers' food"; (2) "Is it not surprising that Black resistance has not yet blown up a schoolbus with white children? They are the softest targets."[20] Allen writes:

Consider the remarks made by . . . Tutu while appearing on . . . WNBC-TV in New York during his last trip to the [U.S.]. . . .

[When asked if, during a civil war, blacks would be worse off,], Tutu replied: "Yes, they (the whites) have the fire power, but we are the domestics. We take care of white people's homes. We cook their food and take care of their babies. Some of the domestics could be recruited and given a vial of arsenic. Who knows what would happen?" Winner of the 1984 Nobel Peace Prize, Bishop Tutu is supposedly a great man of peace. Yet, there he was on television hinting at the callous murder of white children.[21]

None of this bothered the Disciples. In spite of "hate crimes," they still beheld Tutu as "one of God's great gifts to our age." While saying much about "peace," they promote that which is unpeaceful. In January 1986, in observance of the Soweto uprising's tenth anniversary, the Disciples reaffirmed their oneness with Tutu:

> We Disciples, in affirming the centrality of the scriptures [sic] in our life as a people claim that the biblical message calls humankind and all creation toward harmony, peace, justice, and wholeness. With Bishop Desmond Tutu, we recognize that "apartheid says that human beings are created for separation, disunity and alienation." We believe the Christian gospel calls us to be a community of reconciliation which condemns the policy and practice of apartheid as "instrinsically and irredeemably evil."[22]

This statement was made amidst a period of unimaginable horror (September 1985-June 1986). The WCC-sponsored Marxist-Leninist terrorists, as a "community of reconciliation," had been liberating their fellow blacks from the "intrinsically and irredeemably evil" system of apartheid. Calling them "toward harmony, peace, justice, and wholeness," they turned about 600 of them into living, screaming human torches by way of the "necklace method." This was described by Donald S. McAlvany (Council on Southern Africa): "[Those] accused by the revolutionary 'comrades' of collaboration . . . are tried by peoples' revolution courts, held by ANC or UDF [United Democratic Front, i.e., the ANC's internal wing] revolutionaries. The following revolutionary justice is then meted out:

> (1) The terrified victim is captured by his (her) executioners. Frequently his hands are hacked off as a deterrent to resistance. Barbed wire is otherwise used to tie the helpless victim's wrists together. (2) The tire is placed over the shoulders and filled with petrol or diesel. . . . (3) The fuel is ignited with a match. . . . (4) The fuel ignites the tire, which rapidly attains a temperature of 400°C to 500°C. (5) As the tire burns, great clouds of black smoke spiral upwards. . . . [When inhaled, the fumes] destroy the lining of the throat and lungs. (6) The rubber melts and the molten rubber runs down the neck and torso, burning as it goes, deeper and deeper into the flesh and tissue. . . . The victim is now a living corpse. (7) The victim may take up to 20 minutes to die. While he endures this agony, the Comrades stand about laughing and ridiculing him. . . . [The cooked flesh was sometimes eaten.][23]

Still, Reagan showed no compassion. His concern was for the terrorists, or their ideas. Like the Disciples, he too saw apartheid as "intrinsically and irredeemably evil." On 22 July 1986, he said it was the "root cause of South Africa's disorder," calling it a "rigid system of racial segregation, wherein black people have been treated as third-class citizens in a nation they helped to build."[24] That South Africa's original blacks, the Khoisans, were driven out by the xenophobic Bantus (composed of many Central African tribes) was of no interest to him.[25] Never mind that they themselves practice apartheid.

He also demanded that: (1) the "apartheid laws" be eliminated; (2) "all political prisoners [including terrorists] be released"; (3) "Nelson Mandela [a self-avowed

Communist] be released to participate in the country's political process"; (4) "Black political movements [ANC/UDF] be unbanned"; (5) "the Government and its opponents [ANC/UDF/SACP] begin a dialog about constructing a political system that rests upon the consent of the governed."[26] These demands, of course, were part of the sellout process. First, the anti-Communist government is vilified, while its foes are exalted. Then, it is pressured into negotiating, which is usually fatal. To Communists, talking over means taking over.

Two months later (after about 1,700 black businesses, 4,400 houses, 30 churches, and 50 halls had been destroyed by fire, while more blacks were beaten, dismembered, and "necklaced"[27]), Reagan declared: "In the last several months, the South African government, instead of moving further down the once promising road of reform and dialogue, has turned to internal repression." The ANC's internal repression wasn't mentioned. Reagan added: "We all know that South Africa's real problem traces to the perpetration of apartheid. And we know the solution . . . can only be found in lifting the present State of Emergency [which was for the people's protection], repealing all socially discriminating laws, releasing political prisoners and unbanning political parties—necessary steps opening the way for negotiations aimed at creating a new democratic order for all South Africans."[28]

By a "democratic order," Reagan meant a socialistic one, which would later become part of the new world order wherein all nations will have been replaced by what Allen calls "an all-powerful world socialist superstate."[29] This is the very goal of the solidarity revolution, or purpose of the Rocky-Bye/WCC symbiosis.

However, such socialism would actually be communism (i.e., Marxist-Leninist socialism), as implied by an assistant secretary of state (African Affairs), Chester Crocker (CFR), when he said the ANC "has committed itself to democracy." He even called the ANC terrorists "freedom fighters." Yet, the State Department itself saw them this way since, officially, they were considered "the legitimate voice of [South Africa's] Black community."[30]

That Allen's "socialist super-state" would be a Communist one is evident in that Communists are helping to build it. They're part of the solidarity revolution. This is why Communist states are being called democracies, and why communism "is dead." Oh, and the Cold War "is over." (Translation: Opposition to communism has ceased.)

So we see that Reagan's foreign policy was the same as Carter's, which, more accurately, was really Brzezinski's. Reagan must have known this. It was even known to private citizens. One was McAlvany: "[South Africa's] Minister of Police and Justice [told me] in 1977 that the U.S. government was its most dangerous enemy. . . . [He explained how it was] functioning in a clandestine, active support role to the Soviet-backed revolutionaries and terrorist groups throughout southern Africa.

> He [also] described how U.S. funding to these terrorist/revolutionary groups was being directed *through various global and South African church organizations* [emphasis mine] and how the funding conduit for funds channeled to the revolutionaries was through [a certain] U.S. intelligence organization. [Here we see a subversive, joint church-U.S. government operation involving, perhaps, tithes.][31]

That Reagan knew his foreign policy was Carter's is evident in that his policymakers were also Carter's. They would later be Bush's—oh, and then Clinton's. This is why McAlvany calls them the "same old crowd":

> Carter gave away the Panama Canal and sold out Somoza [and the Shaw]. Reagan toppled [Marcos and] is pressuring South Korea to negotiate with [North Korea]. [Meanwhile, his] Administration

is trying to install the Soviet-backed ANC as the next government of South Africa. . . . [These] are the Machiavellian works of . . . the Liberal Eastern Establishment types which have dominated [Reagan] since he won the [1980] nomination. . . . This writer wrote in 1980, citing the French proverb which says, "the more it changes, the more it remains the same," that the same old crowd would still be in control. And they are![32]

By "Establishment types," McAlvany means Rocky-Bye's functionaries, who placed over nineteen nations and about 230 million people under communism since the Vietnam War began—the same fate that awaits us. That is, their new world order is actually the world of communism, "new" only in its totality—and finality. So eventually, under Rocky-Bye, America will cease to exist. For there can either be a super-state or separate sovereign states, but it can't be both ways. Regarding Carter's foreign policy, Rocky-Bye functionary Jeane J. Kirkpatrick (CFR/TC) says, misleadingly,

> its failure . . . is now clear to everyone except its architects, and even they must entertain private doubts . . . about a policy whose crowning achievement was [the giveaway] of the Panama Canal. . . . [This implies that whatever they did was unintentional.] While Carter was President, there occurred a dramatic Soviet military buildup, matched by the stagnation of American armed forces, and a dramatic extension of Soviet influence in the Horn of Africa, Afghanistan, southern Africa, and the Caribbean, matched by a declining American position in all these areas.[33]

Actually, the "failure" of Carter's foreign policy was not failure at all. For, as "its architects" saw it, it was a booming success. What they did they wanted to do since they are still doing it. Besides, any failures could have been easily corrected. As for the "declining American position," it was simply the result of redefining our national interest, as Kirkpatrick herself admits: "[When Carter] came into office it was widely reported that [he] had assembled a team who shared a new approach to foreign policy and a new conception of the national interest. The principal elements of this new approach were said to be . . . the conviction that the cold war was over, and [that America] should give priority to [helping] less developed nations achieve their own destiny." Translation: Abandonment of the containment-confrontational approach, while furthering the Communist takeover of the "less developed [non-Communist] nations." (Later, under a coercive UN, there would be the mandatory merging of all nations.) Kirkpatrick continues:

> More is involved in these changes than meets the eye. [To be sure.] For, unlikely as it may seem, the foreign policy of the Carter administration was guided by a relatively full-blown philosophy of history which includes . . . a theory of social change . . . called [the] doctrine of modernization. . . . [This] doctrine predicted progress (in the form of modernization for all societies) and a happy ending (in the form of a world community of developed, autonomous nations).[34]

Huh? A "world community of developed, autonomous nations"? Now where have we seen this before? Could this be Brzezinski's "community of the developed nations that would embrace the Atlantic states, the more advanced European communist states, and Japan"?[35] But would these nations be "autonomous"? Of course not. Yet, we find both "communities" are indeed Brzezinski's; but, rather than autonomy, they require interdependence, its opposite:

> The administration's approach to foreign affairs was clearly foreshadowed in Zbigniew Brzezinski's 1970 book [*Between Two Ages*]. In that book, Brzezinski [CFR/TC] showed that he had the

imagination to look beyond the cold war to a brave new world of global politics and interdependence. To deal with that new world, a new approach was said to be "evolving," which Brzezinski designated "rational humanism." In the new approach, the "preoccupation" with "national supremacy" would give way to "global" perspectives, and international problems would be viewed as "human issues" rather than [political ones].[36]

Kirkpatrick's description of Brzezinski's so-called "new approach" is without depth. While being critical of his approach, including the related Linowitz/IPS reports,[37] she fails to associate it with Rocky-Bye to which she, Brzezinski, and Sol Linowitz [CFR] belong, even though Brzezinski's "brave new world" is actually Rocky-Bye's new world order, or Gorbachev's "world of communism."[38] Brzezinski himself knows this. He even said "Marxism, disseminated . . . in the form of communism, represented a major advance in man's ability to conceptualize his relationship to his world. . . . It gave [him] a sense of the social dynamic and stimulated a conscious concern with it. [It even] carried . . . an essentially ethical message." Thus, he implies, communism's butchering of over 150 million people was ethical, or an "ethical message."[39] He doesn't explain how such genocide helps people "to conceptualize [their] relationship to [their] world." Perhaps he means only certain people should have this "privilege."

That he does mean this may stem from his ideological affinity with Teilhard de Chardin, the heretical Jesuit priest. "Teilhard," writes Brzezinski, "[notes] that 'monstrous as it is, is not modern totalitarianism really the distortion of something magnificent, and thus quite near to the truth?' " Apparently Brzezinski agrees with this since it upholds his thesis that "Marxism has served as a mechanism of human 'progress,' [though it] has often fallen short of its ideals." So what's a little genocide. After all, it's been the means to an end. Besides, while Marxism hasn't always been pleasant, it "has served to stir the mind and to mobilize human energies purposefully." Also, he adds (Are you ready for this?), it "has decisively contributed to the political institutionalization and systematization of the deliberate effort to define the nature of our era and of man's relationship to history. . . ."[40] Whew!

We can better understand Brzezinski's "brave new world" if we know how he feels about communism, which he says is "the institutionalized expression of Marxism." He is mostly critical of its dogmatism and tendency to oversimplify things. Both of which are due to its "[unwillingness] to accept the notion of the relativity and elusiveness of truth."[41] This, he says, "drives away . . . the 'truth-seeking' and . . . 'efficiency-seeking' intellectuals."[42] Yet, in spite of such criticism, one must not overlook "the major contribution of Marxism [including communism]: its revolutionary and broadening influence, which opened man's mind to previously ignored perspectives and . . . concerns.[43] To say [this, however,] is not to ignore [communism's] enslaving effect . . . or its analytical inability [but] to assert that in the gradual evolution of man's universal vision Marxism represents as important and progressive a stage as the appearance of nationalism and . . . the great religions."[44]

Thus, Brzezinski sees these "isms" as merely stages in the "evolution of man's universal vision."[45] However, he explains, they "have cumulatively [improved] man's political and social consciousness."[46] But Marxism was the most enlightening, having liberated us from all those "irrational beliefs and [dogmatic] institutions" characteristic of "the [dark] age of historical unconsciousness."[47] Well, sort of—until it too became institutionalized. This though was to be expected since the "crisis of institutionalized beliefs is the last stage in the progressive secularization of life [i.e., elimination of institutionalized beliefs]."[48] Then comes "the transition from the tradition of dogma to the condition of diversity [i.e., diversity of beliefs]."[49] Translation: The replacement of nationalism and the great religions (especially Christianity) with a multi-cultural "brave new world."

Actually, it would be no more multi-cultural than the Soviet Union was under Stalin. It would just be—well, the opposite: collectivistic. That is, for the masses—those millions of nameless, faceless non-persons under a brutal, self-serving global nomenklatura (i.e., ruling class whose "two essential functions [would be] administration and the exercise of power").[50] "Culture" then would involve social engineering, slave labor, genocide—and things a lot worse.

To better understand Brzezinski's "brave new world," it also helps to know what he means by "universal vision." While, basically, it concerns how man views his relationship to the universe, Brzezinski sees it as an evolutionary process. One involving the so-called "collective consciousness."[51] Even though he lacks proof of such a thing. So he attempts to validate it by citing Teilhard, who also lacks proof: "There has thus been at work what Teilhard de Chardin has called an 'augmentation of consciousness . . . a stream whereby a continuing and transmissible tradition of reflection is established and allowed to increase.' "[52]

Though Brzezinski might not know it (but probably does), Teilhard is the "high priest" of the New Age movement. Yet he does admit that Teilhard's "popularity [is] symptomatic of our age's need to combine ecstasy with science, mystic belief with knowledge of the material world."[53] And he implies that this "felt need" is also his. So what is it about Teilhard that he likes? Reverend (Catholic) Clarence Kelly (*Conspiracy against God and Man*) provides a possible clue: "Mixing pantheism and socialism, [Teilhard] produced his 'scientific Christianity,' a religion that is neither scientific nor Christian, a mere rehashing of Illuminist 'Christianity.' "[54] Also, writes Texe Marrs (*Dark Secrets of the New*

Age): "[Teilhard] modified evolutionary theory [including] the concept of a further evolutionary stage for mankind—evolution into higher consciousness." That is, mankind gradually becomes "more Christ-like until [it] reaches its ultimate goal: godhood."[55] Kelly adds:

> The least effect of [his] "monistic pantheism" is the spread of belief in a deity that is at best "the synthesis of the Christian God (of the above) and the Marxist God (of the forward)".... As for Teilhard's non-individual, collective consciousness, "to suppose that this impossible fiction could contain something superior to individual personal existence..." is an abominable absurdity; "the idea of a 'superconsciousness' is, in fact, a totalitarian ideal...."[56]

Why is it "a totalitarian ideal"? One reason is obvious. To believe in a "superconsciousness" is a form of self-collectivization. Since to believe in it is also to believe that one is part of it. So for such a person to be independent would be an existential contradiction, which he would know, or feel, in his own way. Thus, having this innate tendency to collectivize himself, he could never know freedom. Yet, though controlled from within, he could also be controlled from without. As Kelly points out, control "of the masses is made possible [through] prior collectivization of their minds."[57] They could, for example, be programmed to believe in a collective mentality, and other pantheistic notions, and then conditioned to behave dependently. This is not hard to do, which is why *that bridge* is still for sale.

Another, more subtle, reason is that these same people could be used to destroy those who resist collectivization, as in New Ageism. That is, they could be further programmed to believe in the spirituality (even divinity) of "their" collective mentality of which they are a part. In fact, being flattering (since to deify it is to deify them), this would be easy. However, as in New

Ageism, such deification would have to be conditional. They would have to become aware of their divine nature in order to acquire "Cosmic [or Christ] consciousness," which leads to godhood.[58] Why? To justify the destruction of those who resist collectivization. You see, then it can be said that having such awareness is of "higher consciousness," which precedes godhood. But not having it is of "lower consciousness," which "[impedes] the evolutionary process toward [godhood]."[59]

Thus not having it is to be inferior, even unfit to inhabit the planet. This is why not having it gets you on the New Age "hit list." Seriously. You're to be Wacoed out when that day comes (i.e., "the Day of Declaration").[60] This is what they mean by "unity in diversity." We must all be like them, even if we're different. As the Hitlerian New Agers see it, there are but two races: (1) their race, the superior one of "higher consciousness"; (2) the other race, the inferior one of "lower consciousness." Marrs notes:

> [It's easy to see] the dangers in a doctrine that artificially creates two races and sets one up as superior. Hitler's poisonous racial theories were not far afield from those of the New Age extremists. The Aryan race was to become the mangod race of a thousand-year [realm] founded by Hitler and his monstrous SS troops. It is no coincidence that, like those of New Age leaders today, Hitler's theories were grounded in the occult and in the teachings of Theosophy and Hinduism.[61]

How does this relate to Brzezinski's "brave new world"? Well, first of all, it's not just his, and it has many other names. Such as (1) "community of the developed nations"; (2) new world order; (3) "world of Communism"; (4) kingdom of God. Moreover, its realization requires a world government or, as Allen calls it, "an allpowerful world socialist super-state." Thus answering our question, Allen explains:

Those in favor of world government resent the influence of the Judeo-Christian heritage and values upon our civilization, but it is important to remember that they are not against religion. Since they realize that their dream of a New World Order must be built on a religious foundation, they seek to replace traditional religions, Christianity in particular, with the religion of Humanism.[62]

So what is the "religion of Humanism"? New Ageism, humanism's spiritual form. That's why it's called "spiritual humanism."[63] While Allen means that humanism in itself is a religion, which is true, it is manifested in many ways—atheistically and non-atheistically. But it despises Christianity: "[Humanists] still believe that traditional theism, especially faith in the prayer-hearing God, assumed to love and care for persons, to hear and understand their prayers, and to be able to do something about them, is an unproved and outmoded faith."[64] Therefore, being "outmoded" (i.e., obsolete), humanists (i.e., those in favor of world government) "seek to replace" it with their own religion. How do we know they're in favor of world government? They say so:

> We have reached a turning point in human history where the best option is to transcend the limits of national sovereignty and to move toward the building of a world community [Brzezinski's "brave new world"]. . . . Thus we look to the development of a system of world law and a world order. . . . [Which would include] cultural pluralism and diversity.[65]

Are we saying that everyone "in favor of world government" is humanistic? No, of course not. Like Allen, we're talking about those who "resent the influence of the Judeo-Christian heritage and values upon our civilization." Most of whom, in a sense, are humanistic. After all, world government itself is. Thus, generally, they are in two categories: (1) secular humanism; (2) spiritual humanism. Former New Age leader Randall N. Baer describes them: "Secular humanism puts man on an earthbound throne of scientific rationalism, self-generated truth, and self-created destiny; spiritual humanism assigns man to a throne that spans the heavens and the earth in a divine heritage of universal lordship, omnipotence, and self-created glory."[66]

This doesn't mean they're in opposition. On the contrary, they work together "in tandem," like a well-oiled machine.[67] Or hand-in-glove, clutched—and bloodstained. Baer therefore warns: "[New Ageism's greatest threat is] that it can . . . be a totally logical rationale for the killing of innocents and the justification of injustice. . . . [Its] logic is: Since the soul is immortal . . . it just keeps reincarnating. [That is, killing people helps to balance out their karma (or cumulative effect of their acts, good or bad) as they evolve toward godhood.]" Baer continues:

> The extremes of secular humanism, as well, can work in concert with . . . spiritual humanism toward modern-day, neo-holocaust dangers. Sound unlikely? Not at all. A neo-holocaust is [occurring] in America today. . . . Abortion clinics . . . have slaughtered over 25-million innocents already. This legalized, sanitized . . . neo-holocaust run by professionals in lab coats . . . should alert us [to the] possibility [of] such horrors [being] extended to other groups. . . .[68]

So this is the force behind the infiltration and subversion of today's Christian churches. Many of these humanists, secular and spiritual, are professed Christians. Yet, whatever they are, their plan "is to take over every Christian church and Jewish temple in the world [and turn them] into centers for the New Age World Religion."[69] How will they do it? Simply by absorbing (i.e., assimilating) them from within, as an apple becomes the worm.

They even admit it's a conspiracy—an "open" one.[70] As also suggested by various New Age book titles: *The Open Conspiracy: Blueprints for a World Revolution* (Wells); *The Aquarian Conspiracy* (Ferguson); *The Secret Doctrine* (Blavatsky); *Toward a World Religion for the New Age* (Davis); *The New Genesis: Shaping a Global Spirituality* (Muller); *Perestroika: New Thinking for Our Country and the World* (Gorbachev). Still, nowhere is it more "open" than at their mega-events. As when New Age promoter Jose Arguelles announced at his 1987 worldwide Harmonic Convergence: "We're almost at the completion stage of bringing . . . the thousands of New Age . . . organizations and churches together."[71]

Even Gorbachev was involved in this event, indirectly. He had also, in 1987, "hosted a gala New Age peace festival, entitled World Congress for Peace, Equality and Development in a Nuclear-Free Environment by the Year 2000," suggesting that New Ageism is much more than just spiritual. In *Perestroika,* says Marrs, he "parroted the standard New Age lie . . . declaring that the drive for world peace 'can and must rally mankind and facilitate the formation of a global consciousness.' A global consciousness is simply a New Age synonym for a One World Mind.

> [He] also called for a "world-wide revolution" so that mankind would have a "new way of thinking." This revolution, he added, must "begin in the mind."
>
> The demonically inspired Soviet chief called for a "restructuring" of the whole world, to include "a new world economic order."
>
> Is [he] really a devout New Ager, or is he shrewdly using the New Age to secretly promote the Kremlin's plans for world domination?[72]

By a "world-wide revolution," Gorbachev means the world solidarity revolution, whose goal is "a qualitatively new world order."[73] Though associated with the "revolution of rising expectations," it is more comprehensive, sociologically.[74] It is therefore more psychological, concerned with man's "inner limits,"[75] which is what Gorbachev means by "a new way of thinking," that is, as defined in the 1977 Club of Rome report, *Goals for Mankind:*

> Inner limits must be expanded; new, more appropriate goals must emerge. We must recognize that the truly critical . . . limits facing mankind today are inner, not outer; they are psychological and political, not physical.

> The desirable new goals for mankind are global . . . yet call for local decisions. The intimate link between the global and the local is the new reality. . . . We must act locally but think globally. . . .

> [Global goals] need to be present in the planning of powerful governmental leaders [e.g., Reagan, Bush, Gorbachev] as well as in the thinking of ordinary people. . . . [For globalism] carries within it the promise of a new world [wherein] all people . . . live with more dignity and greater equality than ever before. . . .[76]

Yes, this is a "promise," so not to worry. But what isn't said is that this "new world" would have a government. That's right—one! A "world socialist super-state." Few of its officials would be Americans, and many of them would be Communists—and New Agers. Such a promise would depend on them. The question then is, would it be kept? Of course not. How could it be? To govern the world would require an extensive ruling class, or global nomenklatura. Would those in this class allow those they rule to be equal to them—and "live with more dignity . . . than ever before"? Why should they? By definition, how could they? The terms "to rule" and "to be ruled" themselves denote inequality.

This is the same "new world" that both the World Council of Churches and the New Age movement call the "kingdom of God," implying that He would be its top nomenklaturist, or Secretary-General, and therefore over the super-state's Politburo and Secretariat (of the Central Committee), like Lenin and Stalin. All of which, of course, is preposterous—unless the WCC, et al., have some other god in mind.

FIVE

Another Dimension

Many non-Christians regard the NCC/WCC complex as truly Christian. Therefore, to them, its association with the Marxist-Leninist world solidarity revolution (i.e., its promotion of "an all-powerful world socialist super-state"[1]) is just as confusing as the established German church's collaboration with the Nazis. This confusion stems from the illusion that the external church (i.e., the physical, organizational structure) and the true body of believers (i.e., "the remnant") are one and the same. But what often passes for Christianity is not Christianity at all. That is, as historian Herbert Schlossberg, (*Idols for Destruction*) explains, "The remnant, under whatever guise it may appear, remains faithful, while in the same organization, society's chaplains bless whatever policy may issue from the civil establishment."[2]

Like big government, which falsely claims to be of, by, and for the people, big church (e.g., the ecumenical movement) pretends to be the true body of believers. Such bigness though (including "organizational unity") is also weakness because of its vulnerability to infiltration and subversion. For example, Schlossberg says that the church "in the Soviet Union could be made part of the state apparatus with little trouble once Stalin had moved his own people into the top leadership. The Nazi revolution similarly found the unified state church easy to take over, while the authorities could deal only with great difficulty with the lay-dominated decentralized churches."[3]

This is happening today, but on an international scale. The "liberal" Eastern Establishment, realizing that a world government "must be built on a religious foundation,"[4] is systematically subverting the church (i.e., replacing it with humanism), which is essential to the fabrication of a world religion. In a sense, this process began with the founding of the Federal Council of Churches (FCC) in 1908. The FCC, as planned, was to be the seed from which a world council would evolve. Actually, as a 1927 House resolution defined it, the FCC was a "Communist organization aimed at the establishment of a state-church."[5] Thus the purpose of the FCC-inspired World Council of Churches (WCC) was to beget, or become, a world-church. Two years after the WCC's founding in 1948, the FCC became the National Council of Churches (NCC). Also, notes A. Ralph Epperson (*The Unseen Hand*):

> The direction of the NCC was no different from that of the FCC. This was revealed in an interview with Gus Hall, the General Secretary of the Communist Party, USA. . . . [He] declared that Communism and the Church [i.e., the NCC/WCC complex] share so many goals that "they ought to exist for one another." Hall [admitted that Communism's plans for the U.S. were] "almost identical to those espoused by the Liberal Church. We can and we should work together for the same things."[6]

But they are working "together for the same things." That's why both Communism and "the liberal church" are in the world solidarity revolution. Along with New Ageism, they make up the largest part of it, excluding the machinery of government. Why then aren't they interconnected? They are. In fact, New Ageism is now part of "the liberal church" in the sense that some of its groups are now members of the NCC/WCC complex (e.g., Anton LaVey's Church of Satan[7] and the Swedenborgians' church of the New Jerusalem[8]). And, that much of "the liberal church" is now using the New

Age bible called *A Course in Miracles*. Texe Marrs says its "influence is especially deeply felt in Unitarian churches and such New Age-oriented denominations as the Church of Religious Science, Unity, and others." He adds:

> However, the course has also caught on with such liberal Christian denominations as the Methodists, Episcopals, Disciples of Christ, and some Lutheran groups. It is also increasingly popular within the Catholic Church. . . .
>
> . . . This is really a set of teachings promoting the basic premises of Hinduism and Buddhism, [and can be thought of] as a doctrinal Hindu/Eastern Mystical text.[9]

Two of the most prominent clergymen associated with the FCC were Harry F. Ward (one of its founders) and G. Bromley Oxnam (one of its presidents). Oxnam also "served as president of the [WCC, 1948-1954]."[10] He had been one of Ward's students at the Union Theological Seminary where Ward was a professor (Christian ethics). Both were Communists. Testifying before the House Committee on Un-American Activities in 1953, a leading Communist party member (Manning Johnson) stated: "Dr. Harry F. Ward, for many years, has been the chief architect for Communist infiltration and subversion in the religious field."[11] This same committee charged Oxnam "with using the prestige of his office to promote Communist causes."[12] This was based on his affiliation with numerous Communist front groups.

The FCC can be ideologically traced to the era of Christian socialism, which began in England around the 1830s. Author David P. Gaines (*The World Council of Churches*) says this era was founded by such Christian Socialists as Frederick Maurice (1805-1872) and Charles Kingsley (1819-1875) who, being opposed to individualism, emphasized "the corporate nature of society and the need for economic, as well as political, solidarity based on the fatherhood of God and the brotherhood of man."[13]

Two of Maurice's disciples were Brooke Westcott (1825-1891) and Fenton Hort (1828-1892), both well-known Cambridge scholars. They were also, along with various eminent clergymen (e.g., Canon Charles Gore, Bishop of Birmingham and, later, Oxford), co-founders of the Christian Social Union and the Industrial Christian Fellowship. Gaines says this movement provided direction to the church's thinking "on social questions, [in preparation for that day when Marxism] would rise to challenge the Christian concept of society."[14] However, it also provided direction for the thinking of those who wanted a "world socialist super-state." That is, they saw this movement as a vehicle, or means, by which their ambitions could be realized. One of them was Oxford professor John Ruskin (1819-1900).

Ruskin, a Platonic idealist, was trained by his mother (a devotee of the old Puritan school) in reading the Bible "of which he read through every chapter of every book year by year."[15] Yet, ironically, his thinking was collectivistic and decidedly anti-capitalistic. Even more ironic since his father, a wealthy merchant, had left him a fortune. Thus, being an Anglophile, he dreamt of doing what Plato, as an Englishman, would have done: establishing "an all-powerful [British-controlled] world socialist super-state." So, while at Oxford, he passed this idea on to his students, most of whom belonged to the upper-crustocracy.

Among them were lord-to-be Alfred Milner (1854-1925) and future South African multi-millionaire Cecil Rhodes (1853-1902), the son of a clergyman. Rhodes was so obsessed with the idea that, many years later, he decided to implement it. However, to do so, he formed a secret society (consisting of three circles) wherein various Oxford and Cambridge men had key roles. It is described by Dr. Carroll Quigley (*Tragedy and Hope*), the late Georgetown University historian: ". . . Rhodes was to be leader; [Lord Milner and two others] were to form an executive committee; [several more aristocrats] were listed as potential members of a 'Circle of Initiates'; while there was to be an outer circle known as the 'Association of Helpers' (later organized by Milner as the Round Table Organization)." As to the Round Table's significance, Quigley notes:

> In 1909-1913, [Milner and his associates] organized semi-secret groups, known as Round Table Groups, in the chief British dependencies and in the United States. These still function in eight countries. . . . In 1919 they founded the Royal Institute of International Affairs . . . [largely financed by] Sir Abe Bailey and the Astor family (owners of *The Times*).

> Similar Institutes of International Affairs [fronts for the Round Table Groups] were established in the chief British dominions and in the United States (where it is known as the Council on Foreign Relations) in the period 1919-1927.[16]

But what does this have to do with Christian socialism? Well, the connection is subtle—but it's there. First, consider the relationship between the British aristocracy and the Anglican Church. It was so close that, until 1828, only members of this church were given top governmental jobs or allowed to graduate from Cambridge or Oxford, Ruskin's alma mater. And, it's still close inasmuch as the sovereign is the church's temporal head, having the right to appoint archbishops, bishops, and other offices. Moreover, Parliament (the legislative governing body) is somewhat influenced by these appointments since the House of Lords includes two archbishops and twenty-four bishops.

So Ruskin and his circle (Sir Abe Bailey, Lord Arthur Balfour, Sir Henry Birchenough, Lord Esher, Lord Albert Grey, Sir Harry Johnston, Lord Alfred Milner, Sir George Parkin, Lord Nathan Rothschild, Sir

John Seeley, et al.) were not isolated from the Anglican Church, nor the Socialist movement. Besides, Ruskin's idea itself was socialistic. That is, he "had persuaded the original Rhodes-Milner Round Table Groups that the way to federate the world was along socialistic lines, i.e., [placing] all property, industry, agriculture, [etc., under a] cadre of financially-controlled political leaders who . . . would compel everyone to do what was good for the new, world-society."[17]

Socialism then was the means by which this "world-society" could be realized and sustained. So was Christianity, especially since almost anything associated with it can be made to seem altruistic—even holy. All of which is why the FCC and WCC were founded and why their founders were Socialists (both Fabians and Marxists). There's also a connection between them and the Council on Foreign Relations (CFR), the U.S. Round Table front—just as England's Christian socialism and America's are related.

However, Christian socialism didn't appear in America until "the late 1880's," after having spread across Europe.[18] This was about the time when some Cambridge aristocrats (dedicated to Ruskin's idea) were "brought into association with Rhodes" by William T. Stead (1840-1912), England's leading journalist, and a social do-gooder. "This association was formally established on February 5, 1891," when Rhodes' secret society began.[19]

Christian socialism originally was a response to the evils of the Industrial Revolution, from which two distinct classes arose: (1) capitalists who—owning land, mines, factories, etc.—invested their money for profit; (2) laborers who—owning nothing—became dependent on the capitalists. These laborers had earlier been producing goods in their homes and small shops—that is, until the capitalists began making them in their factories, and in larger quantities. This, of course, resulted in widespread unemployment, especially since few people were needed to operate the machinery. Thus there was also much job competition, complicated by a willingness to work under any conditions, and the hiring of women and children rather than men due to the simple machine-related tasks. The manufacturing cities soon became centers of poverty wherein jobs were scarce, drinking was rampant, and home life was dismal, particularly since women and children, even under age nine, were forced to work twelve to fifteen hours daily for substandard wages. Though something had to be done about this, the solutions were usually as bad, or worse, than the problems themselves. Especially when they were exploited by forces even more sinister than those causing the problems.

One solution was to create labor unions and trade societies which, having collected dues, engaged in bargaining with employers, a method by which laborers and skilled craftsmen improved their wages, hours, and working environment. Unions also demanded a "closed shop" (i.e., union shop), which prevented the hiring of non-union members. This was crucial to a strike's success when bargaining failed. However, some of these unions were eventually infiltrated by Socialists (including Marxists) and those with criminal records. This led to the misuse of union funds and an increase in bargaining power through violence and threats. Two other developments were: (1) the concentration of economic and political power, e.g., union mergers; (2) the need for union-related legislation.

Another "solution" was labor reform through government (e.g., England's factory acts). Many of England's Christian Socialists were involved in such reform, "seeking a solution to the problems of industrialism, especially those [concerning] the condition of the working classes." They were also active in promoting "the well-being of the laboring classes [e.g., the Workingmen's College and producers' cooperatives]."[20]

Yet, nowhere were Christian Socialists more active in labor reform than in America where most reform-related legislation was at the local level. In fact, at the forefront of such reform was the FCC. So anxious was it to exploit this movement that a survey regarding "the social and industrial conditions of our American people" was introduced at its very first meeting in 1908. Included in this survey was the "Statement and Resolution" (also called the "Social Creed of the Churches"), which "reflected the influence of . . . Josiah Strong, Shailer Mathews, Washington Gladden, Francis G. Peabody, Frank Mason North, Walter Rauschenbusch, Charles Stelzle, and Harry F. Ward." As stated in the survey ("The Church and Modern Industry"):

> There are many phases of the . . . industrial conditions in the [U.S.] which cry aloud for immediate remedy. Multitudes are deprived, by what are called economic laws, of that opportunity to which every man has a right. That to these impersonal causes are added the cruelties of greed, the heartlessness of ambition and the cold indifference of corporate selfishness, [everyone] must with grief and shame admit. . . .
>
> That workingmen should organize for social and industrial betterment belongs to the natural order. . . . Trades unionism should be accepted not as the Church's enemy, but as the Church's ally.[21]

The FCC soon began to "crusade for a shorter working day and week in industry . . . better pay, [and] more favorable physical conditions for labor in factories. . . ."[22] Though, at first, such reform seemed to be its chief concern, it also became involved in international affairs, especially world peace. This was related to its alliance with the Associated Councils of Churches in England and Germany, which was promoting a world peace conference. Moreover, says Gaines, the "chain of events [concerning this conference] had many links, [as the one] forged by Andrew Carnegie [1835-1919], the steel magnate." He continues:

> While attending Kaiser Wilhelm's jubilee in Berlin in 1913, he had been favorably impressed by what he heard of the work of the Associated Councils of Churches in the British and German Empires, and in February, 1914, he offered to establish an endowment of two million dollars to finance a peace program of the churches, on the condition that the Federal Council of the Churches of Christ in America should share in the income and cooperate in the promotion of an international peace conference. To administer the fund, the Church Peace Union was founded in New York.
>
> No time was lost in preparing for a conference. The date appointed for it was August 3-4, 1914, and the place Konstanz, Germany. La Ligue Internationale des Catholiques pour la Paix, a Roman Catholic organization which had been formed in 1911, also decided to meet, August 10 and 11 at Liége, under the chairmanship of Cardinal Mercier. . . . [23]

As a pacifist, Carnegie was merely using "Christianity" to realize his utopian dreams. Besides, believing Darwin and Spencer instead of God, he wasn't even a Christian, which he admitted: "Not only had I got rid of theology and the supernatural, but I found the truth of evolution."[24]

Though born in Scotland, Carnegie was an Anglophile like Ruskin. For instance, he had "an intense belief in the future influence of the English-speaking people, in their democratic government and alliance for the purpose of peace . . . and in the progress of education on unsectarian lines."[25] Thus, like Rhodes (and his scholarships), he backed his ideas with money, giving away about $350 million (which, in purchasing power then, would be like $3 billion today). However, his tax-exempt foundations (e.g., Carnegie Foundation, Carnegie Endowment for International Peace) have long been a source of subversion. That is, they are inter-locked with the other foundations "promoting socialism since their inception."[26] All of which are interlocked with the Council on Foreign Relations (CFR).[27]

The FCC itself was interlocked with the CFR, in the sense that various CFR members were involved in its international agenda, being especially concerned with international justice. For example, having noted the FCC's support for "the Permanent Court of International Justice," Gaines says: "[It] was further reported [in the FCC's 1923 records] that the chairman of the Commission on International Justice and Goodwill, Dr. John H. Finley [CFR], had visited Europe . . .

> heard Lord Robert Cecil on the League of Nations; received from Bankers' Trust Company of New York an up-to-date survey on the economic conditions of Europe . . .

> During the same year a conference on International Relations from the Christian Point of View was held. Copies of the Council's declaration urging membership for the United States in the World Court were sent to all senators, and a World Court Week, culminating in World Court Sunday, was designated. A document entitled *The Churches of America and the World Court of Justice* was prepared, "with the help of such experts as George W. Wickersham [CFR] and Elihu Root [CFR]," and sent to 70,000 pastors. A delegation from the Council waited upon President Calvin Coolidge and Secretary of State Charles Evans Hughes and expressed "what was believed to be the mind of the churches in regard to membership in the Court."[28]

Thus John Finley, George Wickersham, and Elihu Root were all members of the Council on Foreign Relations. While Wickersham was its president from 1933 to 1936, Root (one of its founders) "was its Honorary President from 1921 to 1937."[29] Charles Hughes, who had been a Supreme Court justice twice, ran against Wilson for the presidency in 1916. He had also been an attorney for John D. Rockefeller's (1839-1937) Standard Oil Company, a consolidation of oil refineries and pipe lines. Though Rockefeller's fortune was even greater than Carnegie's, his (and his associates') "methods seemed so ruthless that [he] became one of the most hated men in the business world." And he "never admitted that his actions . . . had been wrong," though "a devout churchgoer."[30]

All of these people were in favor of the League of Nations and the Permanent Court of International Justice (i.e., the World Court), its agency. In fact, "Elihu Root helped to draw up [the Court's] charter."[31] The FCC itself was supportive of the League and World Court, just as the NCC/WCC complex supports the UN and World Court today.

Lord Robert Cecil, a Tory member of Parliament and an Undersecretary of State for Foreign Affairs, was one of the two Englishmen who conjured up the League of Nations. The other was Walter Phillimore, chairman of the Foreign Office Committee. Both were eccentric and also religious. Phillimore, "a well-known ecclesiastical lawyer" (and "prominent in the Church Assembly"), was "an expert on legitimacy, ritual, vestments and church furniture," while Cecil approached "foreign affairs with a strong dosage of religiosity." But they were also "quasi-pacifists who saw [the League] not as a device for resisting aggression by collective force but as a substitute for such force, operating chiefly through 'moral authority.' " Historian Paul Johnson says "President Wilson, tiring of the [Versailles] Treaty negotiations . . . with their necessary whiff of amoral Realpolitik, seized on the League, and made it the vessel of his own copious religious fervor."[32]

Actually, Wilson (who saw the League as "an indispensable part of the peace treaty"[33]) intended to make it "the vessel" of his grandiose ambition: to be, claims Henry Cabot Lodge, the "future President of the World."[34] This ambition was reflected by the last of the "Fourteen Points" in his peace program, published in January 1918: "A general association of nations [i.e., "a world system of financial control in private hands able to dominate the political system of each country and the economy of the world as a whole"[35]]." Wilson's first five points pertained to the abolishment of the "general causes of war" (as through disarmament), while his next eight points concerned " 'self-determination' for Europe." In *History of a Free People*, we read: "Wilson hoped to enlist public opinion everywhere in support of this charter [i.e., the "Fourteen Points"] for a new world order."[36] Behind this, of course, was British-educated "Colonel" Edward Mandell House, Wilson's alter ego and the "chief agent in the formal founding of the Council on Foreign Relations."[37]

Gaines mentions that Finley, while in Europe, had "received from the Bankers Trust Company of New York an up-to-date survey on [Europe's] economic conditions."[38] Bankers Trust was owned by international banker J. P. Morgan (1837-1913), which, says Quigley, was part of the Rhodes-Milner group's "chief backbone," a financial structure "running from [Morgan's New York bank] to a group of international financiers in London [e.g., Lazard Brothers]." In 1901, Milner himself turned down an offer "to become one of the [London Morgan bank's] three partners," as a replacement for J. P. Morgan's son who returned to New York.[39]

The Council on Foreign Relations, a Round Table front, "was [also] a front for J. P. Morgan and Company," and was therefore "dominated by the associates of the Morgan Bank" (e.g., George Wickersham, Elihu

Root).[40] In 1914, the president of the Bankers Trust Company, Benjamin Strong, became the first governor of the New York Federal Reserve Bank, source of the twelve regional banks. "Under Strong," says Quigley, "the Reserve System [was insidiously] brought into interlocking relations with the Bank of England and the Bank of France,"[41] which is understandable since the "original Federal Reserve Board was largely hand-picked by 'Colonel' House," the Federal Reserve Act's "unseen guardian angel."[42]

House, who was Wilson's personal advisor, manipulated him "like a puppet."[43] Moreover, backed by such leading financiers as J. P. Morgan, John D. Rockefeller, Jacob Schiff, and Paul Warburg, House (a financier's son) was largely responsible for the graduated income tax and Federal Reserve legislation being enacted, which fulfilled two of the ten strategic objectives listed in the *Communist Manifesto*.[44] The Federal Reserve System (i.e., a central bank) made it possible for the international bankers, including House's wealthy friends, to finally achieve their goal which—in Quigley's words—was "nothing less than to create a world system of financial control in private hands able to dominate the political system of each country and the economy of the world as a whole. This system," says Quigley, "was to be controlled ... by the central banks of the world acting in concert, by secret agreements arrived at in frequent private meetings . . . ."[45]

The graduated income tax and the Federal Reserve System partially fulfilled House's utopian dream of "an all-powerful world socialist super-state," as described in his book, *Philip Dru: Administrator* (1912). That is, this tax and central bank were indispensable to the creation of what he called "a comprehensive system of state ownership and the leveling of wealth, [which] will lead to socialism as dreamed of by Karl Marx."[46] This is why he set up the Council on Foreign Relations. According to Alan Stang, a well-known journalist:

House founded the C.F.R. to further this purpose, and it has been true to that objective ever since. The purpose of the [CFR] is to collectivize our economy and submerge our national sovereignty in a world government.[47]

This also explains why House and his wealthy associates tried so hard to get the League of Nations covenant ratified during and after World War I. The covenant, which was first drafted by House,[48] was designed to be the prelude to world government. Meanwhile House's associates "were also sponsoring and financing the Communist Revolution in Russia." Allen says the "Bolsheviks were bankrolled by a consortium of bankers, many of them cousins, from Wall Street, London, and Frankfurt." He adds:

> While J. P. Morgan & Company and the Rockefeller interests participated, the chief American sponsor was Jacob Schiff, a senior partner of Kuhn, Loeb & Company and one of the original movers behind the creation of the privately owned and controlled Federal Reserve System. As the *New York Journal-American* reported on February 3, 1949: "Today it is estimated [that Schiff] sank about $20 million for the final triumph of Bolshevism in Russia."[49]

Milner himself contributed to its success, having given the Bolsheviks "over 21 million rubles." Actually, claims one source, the revolution "was engineered by the English." British agents in Petrograd, for instance, were encouraging the soldiers "to mutiny."[50]

After the U. S. Senate rejected the League of Nations covenant on 19 March 1920, House and his associates realized that, in creating a world government, Americans would first have to be conditioned to want one. So, on 29 July 1921, they established the Council on Foreign Relations, which, since then, "has greatly influenced American foreign and domestic policies to fit the designs for world government envisioned by its founders, and has conditioned the American people to accept the changes as both wise and necessary."[51]

This conditioning paid off when on 28 July 1945 the U.S. Senate ratified the United Nations' charter, "virtually without debate." Few "had even bothered to read the thing," says Allen.[52] As to its origin, author W. Cleon Skousen (*The Naked Capitalist*) claims that it "was written by a State Department-Soviet Union coalition of strategists who specifically designed the UN so that it could eventually override the sovereign independence of its member nations and subject them to [its military forces and] the Marxist-dominated World Court."[53] Allen identifies two of these strategists:

> The man termed "the architect of the United Nations Charter" by *Time* magazine [18 May 1953] was Russian-born Leo Pasvolsky (CFR), Chief of the Division of Special Research in the State Department. Born of Communist parents, Pasvolsky was raised a radical and infiltrated into our government in 1934. He rapidly rose to the key position from which he worked to effect the transfer of U.S. sovereignty to the United Nations.

> Working side by side with Pasvolsky in formulating the UN Charter was Alger Hiss, who was at the same time a member of the Communists' Harold Ware cell in Washington, a Soviet espionage agent and a member of the Council on Foreign Relations. . . .[54]

Naturally then the UN's military affairs, including nuclear weaponry, have always been under the Soviets. Yes, always! It's one of the U.S. government's best kept secrets. Why were they given such authority? Two reasons: (1) To give them control over the historical dialectic process; (2) To ensure their control over the military affairs of a world government. This, explains Allen, would be "less embarrassing than merely surrendering to the

Kremlin." Adding: "[This] would solve the PR problem of keeping patriotic Americans from rebelling, [since it] would be sold . . . as a great peace plan rather than a de facto surrender."[55]

So the UN, like its League of Nations counterpart, is a sham, being actually an "all-powerful world socialist super-state" in the making. John Foster Dulles (CFR), involved in both the League and the UN, says it "represents not a final stage in the development of world order, but only a primitive stage." And how does it develop? By simply creating "the conditions which will make possible a more highly developed organization."[56]

By "a more highly developed organization" he means a world government, or Allen's "world socialist super-state," under which the old order (in the non-Communist world) would be replaced by a "new" one (which is what Dulles meant by "the development of world order"), though this "new" one is not really new at all, having been around since 1917—that is, wherever there's communism. Thus, in Allen's words, the UN is also "a front for the international bankers [i.e., "power-seeking billionaires"]."[57] He writes,

> Communism is not a movement of the downtrodden masses but is a movement created, manipulated and used by power-seeking billionaires [and their agents] in order to gain control over the world . . . first by establishing socialist governments [including Communist ones] in the various nations and then consolidating them all through a [merger] into an all-powerful world socialist super-state. . . .[58]

But this "super-state" would have to "be built on a religious foundation," a non-Christian one.[59] In fact, it would have to be the opposite of Christianity: humanism. Why? Because, like Babel, such a state itself would be humanistic. It would also enjoy the status of divinity, requiring the devotion of its subjects. Thus Christians would be persecuted, as in Rome, since their loyalty would be to Christ rather than Caesar. They would seem conspiratorial, resulting in charges of subversion and setting up a state within the state. Moreover, they would be considered non-conformists and a threat to the socio-economic status quo.

This is already evident in that the UN itself is, in a sense, a humanistic temple. William F. Jasper (*Global Tyranny . . . Step by Step*) compares it to the Tower of Babel because of the "rampant idolatry and militant paganism [that] permeate [it]."[60] It even has a Hindu guru, Sri Chinmoy, who actually believes it has a mind, heart, and soul which, respectively, try "to offer flowing Peace . . . glowing Love . . . [and] fulfilling Oneness." Its goal, he adds, "lies not only in thinking together, but in thinking alike."[61] Also, says Chinmoy (as quoted by UN consultant and New Age leader Donald Keys): "The United Nations is the chosen instrument of God. To be a chosen instrument of God means to be a divine messenger carrying the banner of God's inner vision and outer manifestation. One day the world will not only treasure and cherish the soul of the United Nations, but also claim [its] soul . . . as its very own with enormous pride, for this soul is all-loving, all-nourishing, and all-fulfilling."[62]

Keys, who also sees the UN as God's "chosen instrument," writes (*Earth at Omega*):

> Persons who have thought of the United Nations as a
> bastion of atheism, as lacking in spirituality, devoid
> of morals, empty of belief, had better think again.
> They had better wipe their feet and bow their heads
> to enter this First Temple of Humanity.[63]

So only humanism can be the "super-state's" foundation—Christianity's antithesis. Worship of the creation rather than the Creator, which would accommodate all of the religions, while allowing none to be exclusive—equal spiritual opportunity.

The "power-seeking billionaires" (and their agents)

reasoned that since such a foundation could not spontaneously generate itself, it would need an external cause. Thus, under their guidance, the UN was given a spiritual dimension. These "billionaires" also knew that a world government and a world religion, its spiritual counterpart, could evolve simultaneously, each (being complementary) contributing to the other's growth. In this sense, as Dulles disclosed, the UN would be "[creating] the conditions which . . . make possible a [world government]."

Therefore, it was not accidental that the WCC was created shortly after the UN's founding, nor that the UN, apparently, was the only secular outfit to be invited to the WCC's 1948 Inaugural Assembly at which Dulles spoke. Gaines states that "the United Nations Educational, Scientific and Cultural Organization [UNESCO], the International Labor Organization, and the International Refugee Organization [were invited to send] one observer each."[64] Actually then, the UN was being treated as a religious organization. Even though, while the WCC claims to be Christian, the UN represents mostly non-Christians: (approximately) Moslems, 550 million; Hindus, 460 million; Buddhists, 245 million; Confucians, 150 million.[65] That is, more than one billion non-Christians were represented at the Inaugural Assembly of the world's largest "Christian" organization. And they were represented by UNESCO, whose "job . . . is to help create and promote the elements of world citizenship."[66]

It is also not accidental that the WCC and the UN have much in common. For example, like the UN, the WCC was "born a creature of the West," while most of their "founders were from Protestant churches in Western Europe and North America."[67] And even their development was similar, being related to Marxist-Leninist revolution in Asia, Africa, and Latin America. Dr. Ernest W. Lefever (*Amsterdam to Nairobi*) explains that as new "churches from these regions . . . entered the WCC, [its character and] outlook changed. It . . . became more responsive to demands made by church and secular spokesmen from the 'developing' states and by Western representatives who spoke up for Third World causes.

> This development is not unlike that which took place in the [UN's] General Assembly as it increased its membership from the original 60 in 1950 to 149 in 1978. Within the World Council, each delegate has one vote; in the UN General Assembly, each delegation has one vote. Hence both institutions became . . . instruments for the voice and will of their Third World constituencies.[68]

But they were actually "instruments for the voice and will" of the "power-seeking billionaires." They became "instruments for . . . their Third World constituencies" only after they had been assimilated. In the sense that "their . . . constituencies" had become mere extensions, having no "voice and will" of their own.

By incorporating these "constituencies" into the body of the UN/WCC nexus, psychologically and politically, the "billionaires" (and their agents) could foment their "revolution of rising expectations" (as a prerequisite to today's world solidarity revolution).[69] Thus "Christianity" (including liberation theology) and the other world religions were used "to promote its emergence." In 1978, the Club of Rome (*Goals for Mankind*) declared:

> The achievement of world solidarity is the great imperative of our era. It is needed to expand mankind's current inner limits [psychological and political[70]] and prompt the espousal of global goals, bringing long-term benefit. Religions as well as secular modes of thought could, and should, promote its emergence. . . .

> We are in the midst of [a] revolution in consciousness today, activated by the spread of communications and technology. It is a "revolution of rising expectations."[71]

This revolution began long before the Club's report was issued. It was incited by making people in the non-industrialized world want more than they have, or need, as well as to desire what those in the industrialized world have, even though it isn't theirs. But they were told, and still are, that it really is theirs since they're being "exploited for the economic gain of the industrialized world."[72] Oh, and it's because of racism. So if you want what's yours, you'll have to fight for it. However, not to worry—the UN, WCC, and Marxist-Leninist revolutionaries will help you. So let's go for it.

As planned, this resulted "in demands for a new international economic order [NIEO],"[73] the revolution's major objective and (says Lefever) the "WCC's solution for the world's 'maldistribution of wealth' and oppressive structures," even though it "originated in . . . the United Nations," and had Moscow's support, as well as assistance, according to Lefever. He says

> Castro made this point in [a] speech: "The Soviet Union initiated a kind of Christian relation with Cuba that might be considered the New International Economic Order to which we of the world's underdeveloped countries aspire." Justice for the WCC did not mean . . . aid to or investment in the Third World, but rather a forced redistribution of income and resources from rich countries to poor ones [including Communist ones]. . . .[74]

By raising the Third World's expectations, the UN/WCC nexus had been laying the groundwork for the NIEO ever since the WCC's inception, even though the UN didn't call for it until 1974,[75] which was deceptive, considering the UN was already building it with the WCC's help. At least since 1954: "Evanston [i.e., the WCC's second assembly, 1954] anticipated a rise in the [Third World's] standard of living . . . as rich countries made 'increasing sacrifice.' Churches were urged to recruit Christian technicians and administrators to serve in U.N. agencies 'meeting the needs of . . . underdeveloped countries.' "[76]

It was also evident during the next three large meetings: New Delhi Assembly, 1961; Geneva Conference, 1966; Uppsala Assembly, 1968. For instance, Lefever speaks of a New Delhi report that "contained the faint outlines of what later came to be called the New International Economic Order." Some of its topics were: "international economic cooperation, U.N. development aid, [and] fair trade policies." As for Geneva, one of its "principal themes" was "[closing the] gap between rich and poor states," which, says Lefever, "would require a New International Economic Order in which the developed nations would contribute 1 to 2 per cent of their annual GNP to aid the underdeveloped, [and] tariff barriers against the Third World would be removed . . ." Regarding Uppsala:

> To close the gap between rich and poor and to move toward a New International Economic Order, Uppsala followed the lead of Geneva and recommended that by 1971 the industrialized powers increase their Third World development aid to at least 1 percent of their GNP. Church members were urged to impose on themselves a voluntary development tax based on the difference between what their government was giving and what it should give. . . .[77]

So if, as Allen claims, the UN is "a front for the international bankers," then the WCC must be part of it, which is why these bankers and their proxies are associated with it. Some were even at the WCC's inauguration (the Amsterdam Assembly, 1948), including, for example, Prince Bernhard, founder of the Bilderbergers,[78] and John Foster Dulles, a CFR founder. A few others were: John C. Bennett, T.C. Chao, Josef Hromadka, and G. Bromley Oxnam. Gaines mentions that the "Crown Princess [Netherlands] personalized the nation's goodwill and hospitality by attending a plenary session of the Assembly and sitting with the [WCC's] Presidents, in company with her consort, Prince Bernhard. And," says Gaines, "from the Queen at The Hague came the message: 'Owing to the circumstance that the dates of this Assembly coincide with the preparation for the Jubilee, it is impossible for Her Majesty to give at the present moment such attention to the Assembly as she would desire to . . . give, since she follows the work . . . with very deep interest.' "[79]

Also following it with "deep interest" was Dulles, a Presbyterian. Speaking at the assembly, he stated: "In most countries there are important collective and cooperative enterprises. . . . There is no inherent incompatibility between the Christian view of the nature of man and the practice of economic communism or state socialism. . . ." As for Dulles, Gaines adds:

> The program the churches should support is, [Dulles] urged, one for peaceful evolution to international unity. . . . It should be recognized, he suggested, that the long-range social ends which Soviet leaders professed to seek were in many respects similar to the ends which Christian citizens sought . . . "Most of them have been sought by Christians long before there was a Communist party," he declared.[80]

This "Christian" Socialist cliché has long been used to weaken Christian opposition to socialism, which communism itself is. Many Christians fail to realize that socialism "is the ultimate monopolistic system." Rather than being of, by, and for the people, a Socialist state (which controls production and distribution, etc.) is usually "owned" and controlled by a "monopolistic clique behind the scenes" (e.g., the Rockefellers, et al.). And, says Allen, no "competition is allowed." The Socialist state "serves them as a legal holding company with which they merge their competitors under their control." All of which "is done in the name of 'the People,' of course!"[81]

This is why John D. Rockefeller, Jr. (1874-1960), on whose land the UN headquarters was built, was also involved in the Christian Socialist movement. Besides giving over $137 thousand to the FCC during 1926-1929,[82] he gave $100 thousand to the WCC in 1954 for the promotion of "rapid social change" (i.e., revolution) in the Third World.[83] Such change would create an unstable situation wherein Third World nations, including Communist ones, would require economic assistance (particularly taxpayer-backed loans and industrialization) from the developed nations.

By Geneva (1966), whereat "Martin Luther King, Jr., was asked to preach,"[84] both Third World assistance and revolutionary violence "had become . . . a major concern." Then, "on May Day of 1974," the UN (as if to reimburse the Rockefellers for their land) adopted "the 'Declaration on the Establishment of a New International Economic Order.' "[85] It read: "We . . . proclaim our united determination to work urgently for the establishment of a new international economic order based on equity, sovereign equality, [and] interdependence. . . . The prosperity of the international community as a whole depends upon the prosperity of its constituent parts."[86]

About five years earlier, this "rapid social change" project had been reinforced by another, even more pernicious, one: the Program to Combat Racism (PCR), which actually was not to combat it but to create it. This contrived racism inspired the revolutionary fervor needed to change things more rapidly, especially through terrorism. It was said that Third World peoples were the victims of racism, colonial repression, and social injustice. Their distress was blamed on all whites in the industrialized world, particularly South Africa. All were guilty, collectively, without even knowing them—or anything about them. This program, according to Lefever,

was rooted in the strong anti-racism pronounce-
ments of the Uppsala Assembly in 1968 and in a
recognition of the ineffectiveness of the WCC Secretariat on Racial and Ethnic Relations (established in 1961). Its direct impetus was a WCC
consultation held in London in May 1969 under
the chairmanship of U.S. Senator George
McGovern (D-SD), who had been a Methodist del-
egate at Uppsala. [This] London meeting succeeded in issuing proposals to eradicate racism
[such as] economic sanctions against "racist" regimes [e.g., South Africa], and moral and material support for groups [e.g., ANC/UDF terror-
ists] fighting racism.[87]

Yes, that's right. McGovern was a senator then, while
being officially involved in the WCC's affairs—in this case,
its financing of Marxist-Leninist terrorism with tithes! Dr.
Susan M. Huck remarks: "Ever since he pioneered this
business of emptying American church collection-plates
into the pockets of Marxist terrorists in Africa through the
World Council of Churches, back when he was a top
[WCC] functionary . . . McGovern has considered it his
business to destroy the remaining whites in Africa."[88]

But why? Because, says Huck, they "[weren't] part of
the machinery of the New World Order." You see,
McGovern is a member of the Council on Foreign Relations, a key Rocky-Bye agent. That's why he signed the
"Declaration of Interdependence" on United Nations
Day in 1975.[89] It read: "Two centuries ago, our forefathers
brought forth a new nation; now we must join with others
to bring forth a new world order."[90] However, as McGovern
knew, "interdependence is a condition and not a goal," a
condition through which Rocky-Bye's goal, "interexistence," can be pursued. "To interexist," explains the Club
of Rome,

means to pursue one's own goals and aspirations,
achieve one's own pathways of growth and development, and to do so within the framework of an

> interrelated global community [i.e., "world social-
> ist super-state"]. . . .
>
> The logic of interexistence does not require that
> all nations and peoples be alike. . . . Diversity is of
> the essence, in the interests of mutual
> balance. . . . But diversity without coordination
> [i.e., control] can become destructively chaotic [i.e.,
> obstructive].[91]

This kind of "diversity" is seen in a speech by UN Secretary-General Dag Hammarskjold, a Socialist who was "imbued with an exaggerated, humanistic view of his ability to 'save the world,'" even believing he was "'a new Jesus.'"[92] Addressing the Evanston Assembly, about UN/WCC collaboration, he declared: "In spite of . . . differences in character and responsibility, the churches and . . . the United Nations have an aim in common and a field of action where they can work side by side." What is this "aim in common"? Well, the churches and the UN "stand side by side as participants in the efforts of all men of good will, irrespective of their creed or form of worship, to establish peace on earth." After all, the UN "is inspired by what unites and not by what divides the great religions of the world." (So much for diversity.) Then, as to how "peace on earth" can be established, he explains: "[By] helping underdeveloped countries to achieve such economic progress as would give them their proper share of the wealth of the world." In other words, by implementing the NIEO. In regard to "ideological tensions," he felt the church could ease them: "[The] Cross . . . should not separate those of Christian faith from others but should, instead, [enable] them to stretch out their hands to peoples of other creeds in the feeling of universal brotherhood which we hope one day to see reflected in a world of nations truly united."[93]

What is he really saying? Is it that, in the eyes of God, all religions are the same; and therefore Christians shouldn't be so partial to their own? Or is it that Christians should treat non-Christians as though they were Christians?

Both, but what this "new Jesus" had in mind was the "new humanism which embraces all people,"[94] a ritualistic belief system involving worship of the creature rather than the Creator. And a religion "encompassing within [its] sphere of concern and solidarity all human beings, believers and nonbelievers, as well as the faithful of other religions." It would also be an amalgamation of today's religions, which is what the Club of Rome means by "[today's] religions have begun to evolve new forms of humanism." Adding: "[This] coming together of the [religions] is a sign of greater unity within their diversity, not of syncretism and uniformity. . . . [Such] unity . . . is necessary if some of the deepest thoughts and experiences of mankind are not to give rise to the exclusiveness and intolerance that breeds inhumanity and violence."[95]

But was Hammarskjold really trying to prevent "inhumanity and violence"? Hardly. As the UN's high priest, he had perpetrated it himself (e.g., UN "peacekeeping"— Katanga). And he greatly admired Chou En-Lai who, along with Mao Tse-Tung, "[slaughtered] between 34,300,000 and 63,784,000 human beings," which the *Guinness Book of World Records* (1976) calls the "greatest massacre in human history." Yet this "new Jesus" saw Chou as "the most superior brain I have [ever] met in . . . foreign politics." How can this be explained? Well, as "an extreme left-winger," he was ideologically compatible with Chou, both having the same revolutionary cause. Only their roles were different.[96]

Thus religious unity has nothing to do with "[establishing] peace on earth." It's just the opposite: "[promoting] the growth of world solidarity."[97] Meaning that those who pursue such unity are part of the world solidarity revolution, whether they know it or not. But those who know it also know its object is "a qualitatively new world order,"[98] though possibly calling it the kingdom of God.

How would it differ from the old order? Well, first of all, says the Club of Rome, to solve today's problems, "the present world order must transform into one of . . . mutually beneficial cooperation," and this requires the expansion of "mankind's inner limits [psychological and political]," one of the solidarity revolution's major tasks. Then, after this transformation, "the new order would no longer exhibit the tenuous ties of self-centered coexistence but would practice the principles which define [what] we call interexistence [i.e., "existence that is mutual and reciprocal"]."[99]

So by religious unity, the Club means solidarity. Not Christian solidarity but religious solidarity, or, more accurately, world solidarity—the gathering of the masses having been given unity of purpose (i.e., their goal or revolutionary cause). Religious unity then is a means to an end: the kingdom of God (i.e., "a qualitatively new world order"). And those who oppose such unity (e.g., genuine Christians) are said to be divisive, exclusive, and intolerant, being too particularistic. Thus, says the Club,

> [Religious] influence could promote the growth of world solidarity, or it could increase ethnic and cultural disharmony, depending on whether the particularist or the universalist elements of the teachings gained dominance. . . .
>
> . . . [Today, the] spirit of accommodation can grow much more rapidly . . . as common global dangers kindle a fresh appreciation of the universalist elements in all the major . . . religious traditions of man. . . .
>
> . . . All the great religions possess . . . teachings which encourage concern for the future. The eschatology of the monotheistic religions, and the reincarnation doctrines of Oriental thought are examples. . . .[100]

Here the Club is advocating universalism, a sort of spiritual egalitarianism. Wherein everyone is good, and equally so, thus equally deserving of salvation. Meaning they'll all go to heaven—and get a free lunch. Like the Dodo's race in Wonderland, there are no rules, no losers.

> There was no "One, two, three, and away," but they began running when they liked, and left off when they liked, so that it was not easy to know when the race was over. [So when it did end, they asked], "But who has won?"

> This question the Dodo could not answer without a great deal of thought, and it sat for a long time with one finger pressed upon its forehead . . . . At last the Dodo said, "Everybody has won, and all must have prizes."[101]

SIX

Solid-air-ity

The world solidarity revolution, including its revolution of rising expectations, is like an ever-expanding mass of rising hot air. Why hot air? Because it's impelled by lies and deceit. Still, it's even more like a poisonous, hallucinogenic vapor, inducing within its adherents vain hopes and expectations, never to be realized since their destiny has already been prepared.

The term "world solidarity revolution" was coined by Ervin Laszlo, project director of the Club of Rome's fifth report (1978), *Goals for Mankind.* The purpose of this revolution, also called a "world mobilization," is to solve the world's many problems before it's too late.[1] As the Club sees it, the world is "a fragile spaceship" coming apart in midair.[2] For one thing, there are too many people in it, and not enough food, fuel, and other resources for them, since they're destroying it (i.e., the earth) while in flight, along with its cargo (i.e., the resources). And they're even destroying each other (e.g., through the proliferation of weapons, nuclear and conventional).

So how can this spaceship be saved? Well, first of all, its passengers must realize it's in trouble. This requires consciousness raising and spaceship solidarity, a task of "the advance guard," those who "are [already] conscious of global problems and promote global solidarity for resolving them." That is, their function is to "communicate [their] insights to the people."[3]

Does this mean that solidarity itself will save the ship? No, only that solidarity "is needed to expand mankind's current inner limits [psychological and po-

litical] and prompt the espousal of global goals. . . ."[4]
Which lead "to a future that is safer, more equitable,
more humane, and less crisis-prone than the present."[5]
However, this is not what the Club really means since,
several pages later, we read:

> The pursuit and gradual achievement of global
> goals would create a qualitatively new world or-
> der. This order implies correspondingly new re-
> lationships among societies. . . .

> . . . If crises and catastrophes are to be avoided,
> the present world order must [be replaced by one
> that practices the principles of interexistence].[6]

And to "interexist means to [do everything] within
the framework of an interrelated global community,"[7]
which is the "qualitatively new world order," or Brzezinski's
"community of the developed nations,"[8] Solodovnikov's
"world government . . . of a world Socialist (Communist)
community,"[9] and Gorbachev's "world of Communism."[10]
This is why Gorbachev, like the Club itself, warned: "This
world is . . . one whole. We are all passengers aboard one
ship, the Earth, and we must not allow it to be wrecked."[11]
He even refers to it as "a qualitatively new state," as though
having read the report, which he probably did, since V. G.
Afanasiev helped to write it, even explaining how
Gorbachev's ship can be saved: "Only by close cooperation
will the countries of the world be able to solve the global
problems which concern all mankind—such as the protection of the natural environment, the distribution and use
of energy, natural resources, and food reserves. . . ."[12]

So rather than saving the ship, it's to be replaced with
a new one—a slave galley on which we'll all have oars of
equal length, while chained to our seats, collectively,
irrespective of race, nationality, religion, gender, or age.
And there will be free, indiscriminate burial at sea. All this
in "a future that is . . . more equitable."

This Club of Rome report was largely funded by
the U.S. government (National Science Foundation). But

why would "our" government promote a revolution leading to "a qualitatively new world order"—thus undermining its very existence? Laszlo provides a clue: "[The] majority of [my] initial core group spent over a month at the [Aspen] Institute's beautiful Colorado location," having been invited by its president, Joseph Slater (CFR). He adds: "Informal discussions [were held] with many eminent persons, including Harlan Cleveland, Douglass Cater, [and] George W. Ball. . . ."[13] All of whom were members of the Council on Foreign Relations.

At least six other CFR members were also associated with the report: David C. Gompert (international project team member), Robert Triffin, William Watts (project consultants), Richard A. Falk, Saul H. Mendlovitz, Glenn T. Seaborg (distinguished advisors).[14] Seaborg, also a World Future Society member, later sponsored the 1991 World Constituent Assembly (including the Provisional World Parliament).[15] Two other international project team members were New Ager Donald F. Keys and *Pravda* editor V. G. Afanasiev.

Of Aspen's approximately one hundred members (who are either trustees, staff members, or program directors), thirty-three of them belong to the Council on Foreign Relations, six to the Trilateral Commission, and seven to both. A few well-known ones are Douglass Cater (CFR), Umberto Colombo (TC), Shirley Hufstedler (CFR), Henry A. Kissinger (CFR/TC), Robert S. McNamara (CFR/TC), Cyrus R. Vance (CFR), Paul H. Nitze (CFR), Saburo Okita (TC), John J. McCloy (CFR), Richard N. Gardner (CFR/TC).[16]

The Aspen Institute (like the Trilateral Commission, World Federalist Association, et al.) is just one of the Council on Foreign Relations' many "adjunct organizations." That is, the Rocky-Bye-Baby network with which the Club of Rome, Bilderbergers, and other New Agey groups are affiliated, all being used "to promote the CFR viewpoint,"[17] as the CFR-controlled media have been doing.

Rocky-Bye's adjuncts tend to have overlapping memberships, thus sharing many of their members. For example, George Bush is a Bonesman,[18] Freemason,[19] CFR-member, Bilderberger affiliate,[20] and former Trilateralist. He is also a New Ager, belonging to such outfits as the Millennium Society[21] and Points of Light Foundation.[22] UN official Maurice Strong, a New Ager, is another example, being a member of (among others) the World Federation of [UN] Associations, World Economic Forum, Club of Rome, Aspen Institute, World Future Society, Lindisfarne Association, Planetary Citizens, and Business Council for Sustainable Development. He even has his own New Age center, the Valley of the Refuge of World Truths.[23]

Even Aurelio Peccei, the late founder and president of the Club of Rome, was a joiner. Besides being a Bilderberger, he was associated with Planetary Citizens[24] and (along with Laszlo) Donald Keys' Planetary Initiative for the World We Choose.[25] In the Club's *Mankind at the Turning Point* (1974), Peccei "reveals his pantheistic/New Age beliefs, talking about man's communion with nature and the transcendent. . . ." His use of "the term 'noosphere' [concerning] the collective field of intelligence" identifies him "as a student of Pierre Teilhard de Chardin." Author Gary H. Kah (*En Route to Global Occupation*) provides additional evidence of the Club of Rome's overlapping membership: Robert Anderson and Harlan Cleveland "are members. Both men belong to the CFR and have been closely associated with the Aspen Institute for Humanistic Studies. Four of our U.S. congressmen are members, along with representatives of Planned Parenthood, officials of the United Nations, and people connected to the Carnegie and Rockefeller foundations."[26]

Cleveland was one of the "eminent persons" with whom Laszlo and his "initial core group" conferred at Aspen. They "aided immeasurably," says Laszlo, "in crystallizing the basic concept of the research tasks. . . ."[27]

However, Cleveland's contribution relates to his *Agenda for the Planetary Bargain* (1975), which the Club of Rome report includes in its references, parenthetically listing his topic as "Development Goals," which is covered in the report's chapter fifteen. What are these goals? Gary Allen reveals nine of them:

1. Create a World Food Bank.
2. Provide for international control of all sources and supplies.
3. Internationalize commodity markets.
4. Establish international control over the wealth of the oceans and deep seabeds.
5. Provide for international control of the 'weather at human command.'
6. Rewrite the rules of trade and investment.
7. Create a world currency.
8. Create a world police to 'keep the peace when it is threatened and restore the peace when it is broken.'
9. Provide special programs to teach the benefits of the New World Order to each of six 'categories of American institutions,' namely: business, corporations, labor unions, non-profit enterprises, communications media, educational systems and government agencies.[28]

Cleveland refers to his goals as "a complex agenda of international action," which, he says, "amounts to a third try at world order [since the UN is] unable in its present condition to cope."[29] This, of course, implies that it would "try at world order" if it could, and that it should were it able to.

He also sees "a distinction between the future of the [UN] and the future of world order."[30] But, rather than their "future," he really means them (the UN and world order) since, though different, they're not unrelated. That is, the difference is in their cause-effect relationship: the UN (a potential world government) is a causal (and controlling) force by which "world order" can be realized (and sustained). However, in itself, it is not yet such a force since it must operate subversively, via "outside" agents and organizations. Thus, today, there is no "world order," only disorder: cultural atrophy and socio-economic entropy in the wake of the world solidarity revolution whose modus operandi is *ordo ab chao*.[31]

Allen says the CFR initiated "a special program . . . called the '1980s Project' " on how to achieve Cleveland's agenda or "third try at world order." Involved in it "were Henry Kissinger, Cyrus Vance, Theodore Hesburgh, Paul Volcker . . . and other CFR-TC dignitaries." Later on, Harold Brown (CFR/TC), Carter's defense secretary, told the Trilateralists "that new leadership and new plans were required 'for transition to the world of the year 2000.' As a result, Robert O. Anderson of Atlantic Richfield Oil, Aspen Institute, [Club of Rome], CFR, etc., [formed] a 'Committee on the Year 2000,' which is designed to provide that new leadership. . . ."[32]

So, in a sense, the Rocky-Bye-Baby network, and its affiliates, are, collectively, an extension of the UN, particularly its headquarters. Were the UN a large octopus, a milli-UNopus, they would function as its brain. While its tentacles would be, among others, the liberal-left churches, New Age groups, and non-governmental organizations (NGO's). Together, all of these entities, along with international socialism/communism, represent today's major revolutionary force; and, including its millions of dupes (the UNopus' suckers), it's called the world solidarity revolution.

This explains the Club of Rome's UN connection. Even Laszlo was "a Senior Fellow at the United Nations Project on the Future at UNITAR" (United Nations Institute for Training and Research).[33] And he admits that an office for his *Goals for Mankind* report "was established at UNITAR," which was at "the invitation of Davidson Nicol, UNITAR's distinguished Executive Director, and on the initiative of Philippe De Seynes, head of the Project on the Future." He adds: "This office . . . proved to be invaluable both for handling the complex logistics of research coordination and providing access to experts and leaders [worldwide]."[34]

Actually this report (1978) is a revision of an earlier one entitled *Goals in a Global Community: Original Studies of the Goals for Mankind Report to the Club of Rome,* edited by Ervin Laszlo and Judah Bierman (Pergamon Press, 1977). The difference between them is that "fresh original materials have been added" which, states Laszlo, do two things: (1) "update the 'World Atlas of Contemporary Goals' by taking account of new goals emerging in the United States, the European Community, the People's Republic of China, and India"; (2) "provide a more penetrating assessment of the adequacy of current goals, and follow up the discussion of the World Solidarity Revolution by outlining the kind of social and international relations that would constitute essential features of the new world order."[35]

By "goals," Laszlo means "goals of the different regions, ideologies, and religions of the world," including "governments, business corporations, religious groups, intellectuals, and [even the ordinary] people." By "adequacy" of these goals, he means their sufficiency for solving "global problems."[36] That is, they should be either global or, at least, accommodative, which is why it is necessary "to reconcile short-term [national] realities with long-term [global] needs," those which a new order would fulfill. Thus, says the report,

> if our goals are unrealistic . . . world problems will lead to catastrophes, while if they are realistic . . . new horizons of need fulfillment and peace can open for the world community. . . .
>
> . . . [Modern] society is caught in a race in which its own survival is at stake—a race between the eruption of global problems and a world mobilization [i.e., solidarity revolution] to meet them before they become . . . intractable.[37]

But does "to meet them" mean to solve them? No, this is misleading. Only a new world order can do that. And there can't be one until our global consciousness has been sufficiently raised (i.e., inner limits enlarged) by the solidarity revolution. Because this would enable the old order to be transformed into a new one: "If . . . catastrophes are to be avoided, the present world order must transform into one of active and mutually beneficial cooperation [i.e., interexistence]. In the wake of a world solidarity revolution, mankind's [psychological and political] inner limits would be sufficiently enlarged to permit such transformation."[38]

All of this jibes with Brzezinski's views. Several years earlier, he mentioned the "transformation . . . now taking place, especially in America, . . . creating a society increasingly unlike its industrial predecessor,"[39] which is due to the "global human conscience [that is] beginning to manifest itself,"[40] and "an awareness that the basic issues facing man have a common significance for human survival, irrespective of international internal diversity." Thus the "concern with ideology is yielding to a preoccupation with ecology," such as "the unprecedented public preoccupation with . . . air and water pollution, famine, overpopulation, radiation, and the control of disease, drugs, and weather, as well as in the increasingly non-nationalistic approaches to the exploration of space or of the ocean bed." Translation: "The new global consciousness [is becoming] an influential force," which is necessary since, if the spaceship is to be saved, the old order must be transformed.[41]

So, happily he writes: "Today the framework [i.e., traditional cultures, religions, and "national identities"] is disintegrating." However, unhappily: "The new global unity [i.e., solidarity] has yet to find its own structure, consensus, and harmony."[42] Then, happily again: But "there is still a felt need for a synthesis that can define the meaning and historical thrust of our times," a need associated with "equality," which "motivates both the rebels in the universities . . . and the new [Third World] nations in their struggle against the . . . richer ones [i.e., non-Communist Western countries]."[43]

Here Brzezinski connects the campus-based cultural revolution with the revolution of rising expectations (including its New International Economic Order, NIEO). He claims they seek "equality." And later connects them again through their association with "rational humanism," which relates to global consciousness. That is, he explains, "rational humanism is expressed in several ways: first, in an emerging international consciousness that makes so many Americans . . . go beyond purely nationalistic concerns and become deeply involved in global problems . . . and is prompting in American youth [a] preoccupation with problems of ecology; second, in a growing tendency [not] to view international problems as . . . political confrontations between good and evil. . . ."[44]

An example of the first is the NIEO. He says "the principle" of aiding the Third World "is a new moral position and . . . an important component of the new global consciousness." Also he says that while most nations contribute "less than one per cent of their GNP . . . they have in effect created a binding precedent: the extension of aid has become an imperative."[45] He presumably feels it is moral to transfer someone's earnings (through taxation) to people in other countries, even Communist ones. But, of course, under his rational humanism, evil is to be ignored—or redefined.

As for the cultural revolution, he says "rational humanism is part of [it]." Meaning that the revolutionaries were (and are) globally conscious. (Since such humanism "is expressed" by global consciousness.) He also asserts that the revolution's "positive potential . . . lies in its promise to link liberty with equality." A linkage that was "hindered by deeply embedded fundamentalist religious values." He then explains (sort of) how liberty and equality can be joined:

Linked to political reform, the current cultural revolution could gradually enlarge the scope of personal freedom by increasing the sense of self-fulfillment of an unprecedented number of citizens and give greater meaning to equality by making knowledge the basis for social and racial egalitarianism. [Whatever that means.] It could create the pre-conditions for a socially creative and individually gratifying society that would inevitably have a constructive world role to play.[46]

But why would such a "society" need a "world role"? Can't America, or any other country, be "creative and . . . gratifying" apart from the rest of the world? And what do "liberty and equality" have to do with it? Actually nothing, unless, as in Brzezinski's mind, they are associated with his rational humanism and its global ends. Such humanism, he says, doesn't "involve . . . universally prescriptive concepts of social organization but stresses cultural and economic global diversity."[47]

What does he mean by "diversity"? Well, first of all, Brzezinski thinks like the Club of Rome and therefore relates this concept to interexistence (i.e., "an existence that is mutual and reciprocal"[48]). Meaning it must be controlled—or kept from being too diverse. Since "diversity without coordination can become destructively chaotic." But "with coordination [it] can bring all the benefits conferred by the . . . achievement of global goals." For it "calls . . . for positive interexistence and entente."[49] Such diversity then is collective. That is, it's all right to be different provided you're like everyone else. The Club explains:

> [Existence] cannot be pursued in independence from one another, [nor need it] be pursued in helpless forms of mutual dependence. To interexist means to pursue one's own goals and aspirations, achieve one's own pathways of growth and development, and to do so within the frame-

work of an interrelated global community. The aim is growth and development; the means enlightened cooperation. The outcome is "collective self-reliance"—the self-reliance of each within a harmonized system of mutually beneficial relations.[50]

Thus Brzezinski's community of the developed nations (i.e., the Club's "qualitatively new world order") would be like "an interrelated global community" of anthills. Wherein we would be the workers. And, except for defects, the only diversity would be in the division of labor—excluding, of course, the authorized differences among our masters, the controllers, and the unauthorized ones such as those unseen, even our thoughts (i.e., thought crimes), and activities outside of "the framework of [the] interrelated [hills]." This would also include the relative privacy of our quarters, as in Winston's case (Orwell's *1984*) when he "kept his back turned to the telescreen," or sat to "one side of it [in the] shallow alcove."[51]

So in Brzezinski's community of the developed anthills, everything would be collective. There would be collective diversity, collective liberty, collective equality, and collective consciousness, including guilt. In fact, even our self-reliance would be collective, illogically enough. Though the Club sees it as an "outcome" of interexistence,[52] which implies that existence itself would be collective. Says the Club: "[Through solidarity, the] world would change from an arena of [insecurity] to a global society of undiminished diversity but firm collective self-reliance, greater security, and more equity."[53] But why collectivize it? Because, declares the Club, our destiny is also collective. And we better believe it: "Individuals and organized groups must recognize that they are not abstract and separate from one another. Their actions mutually influence one another, and the sum of their actions determines the future of their over-all system of relations—their collective destiny."[54]

Such "self-reliance" then is not reliance upon the self but rather upon the constituent part of a collectivistic, societal whole. Wherein the self is an abstraction, a Brzezinskian idea, or product of ideation whose only reality is being the means to some end, such as Brzezinski's community.

This is Orwellian of course. For there would be no self. Only "the Party" (i.e., global nomenklatura) would exist: the "Inner Party" and the "Outer Party," over which would be "Big Brother." And as Party members, "under the eye of the Thought Police," we would be required "to say that black is white when Party discipline demands [it]." But actually we would have "to believe [it, or even] know [it], and . . . forget that [we have] ever believed the contrary."[55] Winston, resisting such illogic, asks Inner Party official O'Brien if Big Brother really exists:

> "Of course he exists. The party exists. Big Brother is the embodiment of the Party."
>
> "Does he exist in the same way as I exist?"
>
> "You do not exist," said O'Brien.
>
> Once again the sense of helplessness assailed him. He knew, or he could imagine, the arguments which proved his own nonexistence; but they were nonsense, they were only a play on words. Did not the statement, "You do not exist," contain a logical absurdity? But what use was it to say so? His mind shriveled as he thought of the unanswerable, mad arguments with which O'Brien would demolish him.[56]

Winston's spirit was eventually broken in the dreaded "Room 101," located in the windowless Ministry of Love building. A sort of Lubyanka, the KGB prison on (and under) Moscow's Dzerzhinskii Square.[57] " '[Where] blood flowed [and] where they crushed your soul.' "[58] So upon release, Winston knew with absolute certainty that he didn't exist—and that he even "loved Big Brother."[59]

The setting in *1984* is Oceania which, socio-politically, is not unlike the various Communist countries. Especially since, in Orwell's words: "Collectively, the Party owns everything in Oceania, because it controls everything and disposes of the products [including people] as it thinks fit." That is, like the Soviet Union, Oceania is both oligarchical (i.e., ruled by an elite) and collectivistic, which is natural since collectivism is "the only secure basis for [an] oligarchy."[60] This allows it to be monopolistic and to enjoy high prices, with low quality.

This could also be a description of Brzezinski's community—the same oligarchical, collectivistic, monopolistic system known to man since the beginning of civilization, and thus is not a new order but an old one. Except for one thing: it would encircle the earth, leaving no room for rival systems or for refuge.

There would be one country, having one political system, with one party. And, of course, a "Big Brother," along with his ministries of Truth, Peace, Love, and Plenty.[61] Including "Thought Police"—and a "Room 101," to ensure solidarity, or unity in mind and purpose. Since, explains O'Brien, "[Reality] is not external. [It] exists in the human mind. . . . Not in the individual mind [but] only in the mind of the Party, which is collective and immortal."[62]

SEVEN

The New Oceania

All Communist countries are a kind of Oceania, since they are oligarchical, collectivistic, monopolistic, and have "Thought Police." Yet they're but prefabricated units with which the ultimate, more Orwellian Oceania can be built—that is, the new one (or non-fictional one) comprising all of today's collectivist societies, and any future ones. But what about the others—like America? Well, they're to be assimilated, or absorbed, into the collectivist tradition, which is what the Club of Rome means by "the present world order must transform into one of active and mutually beneficial cooperation [i.e., interexistence]."[1] And also what V. G. Afanasiev means in the Club's *Goals for Mankind:* "[The Soviet Union's] main thesis [is] to use the support of the might, solidarity, and activity of world socialism and its firm alliance with all progressive and peace-loving forces to [move] from 'Cold War' to peaceful coexistence [actually interdependence] with states of differing social structures; a turning point from [hostility] to détente [actually entente] in normal, mutually beneficial cooperation [i.e., interexistence]."[2] This partly defines the Club's "qualitatively new world order": "Due to the active pursuit of global goals, the new order would no longer exhibit the tenuous ties of self-centered coexistence but would practice the principles which define a new concept we call interexistence."[3]

Here the Club goes Afanasiev one better. Even admitting that its "new [world] order would . . . practice the principles [of] interexistence." Though to do this would require something much cozier than détente. What could it be? The Club explains: "Détente is important for

now, but not enough in the long run. [Instead,] we must
have entente: understanding and agreement among
peoples and nations."[4] OK, but what about coexistence?
Well, that would be replaced with interdependence. However, asserts the Club:

> [Interdependence] is a condition and not a goal,
> [so] mankind must find a goal that it can pursue
> through interdependence, and beyond it. Such a
> goal, in fact a goal of goals, is interexistence.

> . . . [Which] means to pursue one's own goals and
> aspirations [collectively], achieve one's own path-
> ways of growth and development [collectively],
> and to do so within the framework of an interre-
> lated global community.[5]

Would Afanasiev agree with this? Why, of course.
It's what the Soviets have always wanted, and why they're
part of the solidarity revolution—the purpose of which
is "a qualitatively new world order," which "would practice the principles [of] interexistence." That is, "an existence that is mutual and reciprocal," or collective.[6]

Thus, under this new order, our "future [would be]
safer, more equitable, more humane, and less crisis-prone
than the present."[7] Meaning there would be "world
peace"—the ultimate goal of the Communist party of the
Soviet Union (CPSU):

> The foreign policy aims and goals of the CPSU
> are organically tied with its domestic policy goals.
> Safeguarding favorable peaceful conditions for the
> building of socialism and communism, and safe-
> guarding universal peace and the safety of the
> nations on our planet—these are the general and
> unchanging aims. . . .

> Therefore, the struggle for communism, waged
> by the Communist Party of the Soviet Union, is
> intrinsically bound up with the struggle for peace
> in the world. In other words, communism and
> world peace are inseparable.[8]

None of this bothers the Club. Why not? Three reasons: (1) "The emerging expectations and demands [of the people, including East Europeans] center on the present and do not conflict with the [CPSU's] long-term goal of [establishing] socialism and eventually communism"; (2) "[There] is a definite tendency [for Communist parties] to put off [the] realization [of their goal] into a vague and distant future"; (3) "[There] is an ongoing dialogue between the official long-term goals of the Communist . . . parties and the immediate aspirations of the people. [Which influences government] policies and socio-economic behavior."[9] Translation: Actually the people in these Communist countries, being free and unoppressed, are an influential force. So if they're not worried about communism, why should we be? Besides, we're all in this "fragile spaceship" together, and only through "mutually beneficial cooperation" can we save it.

No mention is made of the nomenklatura. It simply doesn't exist. There are only two groups: "[The] Communist and Workers' parties" and "the people." Even though the nomenklatura comprises about 1½ percent of the Soviet population—and "proclaims itself to be 'the leading and guiding force' in the country."[10] And though work for "the people" (or non-nomenklatura) is compulsory, while "pay and working conditions are laid down by the nomenklatura alone." Also, notes Michael Voslensky (*Nomenklatura*): "[It] is impossible to get away from the nomenklatura employer. Changing jobs merely means changing from one of its representatives to another. There is no escape from this within the frontiers of the country; for the nomenklatura state is omnipresent, and it has deliberately blocked all routes to work that is not for it—and going abroad is impossible."[11]

The Club also fails to mention the Soviet "Thought Police"—that is, "the secret police (KGB) and the agencies controlled by the Ministry of Internal Affairs (MVD) which is responsible for the supervision of the camps." All of which "belongs . . . to the nomenklatura."[12] To the Club, therefore, these "Thought Police" are also nonexistent, as are their "camps." Even though there are "more than 2,000" of them: slave labor camps, prisons, and psychiatric "hospitals" wherein ordinary people (including women and children) are tortured, humiliated, and overworked. Avraham Shifrin, a former prisoner himself, describes them: "We are speaking of innocent human beings persecuted for thinking differently; reading 'forbidden' philosophical, political, or religious books; posting up notices; putting up a flag; demanding religious instruction for their children; or undertaking a private commercial initiative. These are the 'crimes' for which a Soviet citizen can be imprisoned."[13]

So rather than "the people," the Club must mean the nomenklatura, since "the people" have no power—and no freedom. And since it's the nomenklatura, and not "the people," who are "building . . . socialism and Communism, and safeguarding universal peace," while using "the people" to help them. But this "building [of] socialism and Communism" is also the "building" of the new Oceania, which is Rocky-Bye-Baby's "qualitatively new world order," under what Gary Allen calls "an all-powerful world socialist super-state."[14]

This is why Rocky-Bye (including the Club, its affiliate) sees nothing wrong with having Communist countries in its new order, and thus Communist officials in its "super-state," with their "Thought Police." Yet it speaks of "a new world in which all people could live with more dignity and greater equality than ever before in history,"[15] without explaining why those under communism would be better off than they are now. Still, as its history shows, this has always been Rocky-Bye's dream. But why? Well, says Allen,

> if you want a worldwide monopoly, you must control a world socialist government. That is what the game is all about. "Communism" is not a movement of the down-trodden masses but is a

movement created, manipulated and used by power-seeking billionaires in order to gain control over the world . . . first by establishing socialist governments in the various nations and then consolidating them all through a "Great Merger" into [a super-state].[16]

Thus these "socialist governments" were set up for a purpose. Yes, each for the same purpose, meaning there's a plan to consolidate them (like prefabricated sections) into one body, standardized in accordance with the *Communist Manifesto's* ten planks, which are also used in standardizing (and assimilating) the rest of the world. All of which is in preparation for "a 'Great Merger' into [the new Oceania]," or Brzezinski's "community of the developed [anthills]," which he says "must . . . be formed if the world is to respond effectively to the increasingly serious crisis that . . . threatens [it]."[17] (Translation: The "spaceship" must be saved and this is the way to do it.) But it has "to be [done] piecemeal [i.e., sneakily]," probably requiring "two broad and overlapping phases." That is, he explains, "The first of these would involve the forging of community links among the United States, Western Europe, and Japan, as well as with other more advanced countries [e.g., Australia]. The second phase would include the extension of these links to more advanced Communist countries [and eventually the other red anthills].[18]

It is only fitting then that this Rocky-Bye wiz would have nothing but praise for Marxism. Though he is somewhat critical of its institutionalized form, communism, but only because it "[stifled Marxism's] creativity" and "[diminished] its influence."[19] Yet even this wouldn't have been so bad if it hadn't come "too early and too late." For if it had come at the right time, it could have been "a source of true internationalism," and wouldn't have lost "its humanist appeal," which was a "tragedy," he says, lamentably. Especially since it ended up "in the halfway house of Russia," having missed "its moment of opportunity" in either the "West [or] East."[20] Implying that its being in the West would have made him happy, were it truly international (which it is). As for Marxism (the non-institutional kind): It "represents a further vital and creative stage [following the stages of religion and nationalism] in the maturing of man's universal vision [i.e., "consciousness of a common human fate," etc.]." Also:

1. It is "a victory of the external, active man over the inner, passive man and . . . reason over belief."

2. It "stresses man's capacity to shape his material destiny [and helps him to] understand his reality."

3. It "[expanded] popular self-awareness by awakening the masses to an intense preoccupation with social equality [while] providing . . . moral justification for . . . it."

4. It "represented . . . the most advanced . . . method for analyzing . . . social development."

5. It "appealed . . . to man's ethical, rational, and Promethean [i.e., Prometheus-like or heroic] instincts."

6. It "served as a mechanism of human 'progress.' "

7. It "served to stir the mind and to mobilize human energies purposefully."

8. It helped "to define the nature of our era and . . . man's relationship to history."

9. It "represents [in the "evolution of man's universal vision"] a stage [that is just as important as] nationalism and . . . the great religions." (The synthesis of which will be, or should be, rational humanism.)[21]

The Club of Rome likes Marxism too, even seeing it as potentially useful "to the transcendence of [man's] inner limits and the growth of world solidarity." And, of course, it is since, in a sense, the solidarity revolution is Marxist. However, the Club gives the impression that Marxism is innocuous, even beneficial, as Marx himself was. After all, he "stood for the equality of all people regardless of nationality, race, or sex." And therefore wanted them to have control over, uh—well, everything, especially "the means of production" since this would "restore the dignity of work and liberate [them] from social and economic injustice." So it's only natural that today's Marxists would want "a responsible and valid role in [solving] global problems." And in "seizing global opportunities [through interexistence] with societies based on similar as well as different social and economic principles."[22]

So what's this got to do with "the transcendence of [man's] inner limits"? Well, as Marxists know, they have to be expanded, since they determine his goals. But right now (like his goals) they're too "self-centered, short-term, [and] parochial," which was OK, says the Club, "when resources were cheaper and more abundant, when the environment was unthreatened, when the scale of technologies was smaller, and when nations, cultures, and economies were relatively independent of one another." However, things have changed, and our old way of thinking is no good. So we have to transcend—or expand—it. Otherwise our goals will be too narrow for "our interdependent and highly crowded, technology-obsessed and resource-hungry world." As the Club puts it:

> Inner limits must be expanded; new, more appropriate goals must emerge. We must recognize that the truly critical and urgent limits facing mankind today are inner, not outer; they are psychological and political, not physical.
>
> The desirable new goals for mankind are global in scope yet call for local decisions. The intimate link between the global and the local is the new reality facing mankind. We must act locally but think globally.
>
> . . . [For thinking globally] carries within it the promise of a new world in which [we] could live with more dignity and greater equality than ever before. . . .[23]

But wait! Something's wrong here. If there's to be a "community of nations," why not think nationally? Wouldn't it be better for the "community"? The UN thinks so—or did. According to its 1974 Declaration . . . on the Establishment of a New International Economic Order: "The prosperity of the international community as a whole depends upon the prosperity of its constituent parts."[24] But later—Presto! It was just the opposite. For now the UN flip-floppishly promotes the "think globally" concept, implying that the prosperity of the community's "constituent parts" depends upon the prosperity of the "community." Yet, what's the "community" without its parts? How could there even be one?

There couldn't, if it's international, which it isn't—or wouldn't be. That is, by definition, being a super-state, it would be the only state in the world, a fact most people choose to ignore. Why? Because, apparently, they prefer to believe a lie, like the frenzied, programmed mobs during the French Revolution, whose "inner limits" had been expanded. So, similarly—in our pantaloons, sabots, and liberty caps—we find ourselves parroting "liberty, equality, and fraternity," as the tumbrels rattle down the streets with bumper stickers on them reading "Think Globally."

Thus Rocky-Bye's "community" is simply the world's population collectivized, being under the "socialist governments" that have been consolidated "through a 'Great Merger' into [a super-state]." The new Oceania—oligarchical, collectivistic, monopolistic, despotic, and militarily unchallengeable. Unchallengeable because of Rocky-bye's "disarmament" objectives as disclosed in its secretive State Department Publication #7277: "The over-all goal of the United States is a free, secure, and peaceful world of independent states [i.e., "community of nations"] . . . a world which has achieved . . . complete disarmament . . . and a world in which [everything is] in accordance with . . . the United Nations." So, to achieve this goal, there must be a "disbanding of all national armed forces and [a ban on] their reestablishment in any form [except] those required [for] internal order and [the UN's use]."[25]

There are many problems with this. Three of which are: (1) it's unconstitutional; (2) we would be defenseless; (3) whoever controlled the UN would have control of us—and the rest of the world, since the UN would be the world's most powerful military force. Thus the primary purpose of Rocky-Bye's "disarmament" program is to arm, not disarm. That is, to transfer arms from the nations to the UN so that "no state would have the military power to challenge [it],"[26] which is already happening. The greatest and most outrageous con game ever pulled: world conquest through the stupidity of national leaders who voluntarily, and illegally, surrender their military forces to a foreign power for its promise of "peace," which they already have, or can have. Adam Weishaupt was right: "Oh! men, of what cannot you be persuaded?"[27]

Actually Weishaupt was gloating over the success of his false new religion, "Masonic Christianity,"[28] or Illuminism, which even leading clergymen, and academics, were accepting, believing it to be the real thing. As Weishaupt exclaimed: "The most wonderful thing is that [they] still believe . . . it contains the true and genuine spirit of the Christian religion."[29] Yet, even more "wonderful" is that many intellectuals today also believe this, proving that one can be both "educated" and ignorant at the same time, while also being illumined, even though Illuminism is a formula for totalitarianism: pantheism/naturalism + anarchism = political collectivism. Yet it is also the recipe for making an Oceania. Rev. Clarence Kelly (*Conspiracy Against God and Man*) explains:

> [Weishaupt's] two chief collectivist doctrines . . . were anarchism and pantheism, the doctrines of political and religious collectivism—anarchism being his attack on property and legitimate civil authority . . . and pantheism, his attack on the Judeo-Christian God, organized religion, and objective morality.

> . . . It [is] plain, we think, (1) that Weishaupt's
> "Christianity" is fundamentally identifiable with
> the new theology of so-called "Liberal" Protes-
> tantism and "Catholic" Modernism; and (2) that
> the substance of Communist ideology is the same
> as that of the Illuminist political ideology.[30]

Why is pantheism antithetical to Christianity? Because it denies God's existence, or redefines Him. How?
Simply by equating Him with the universe, including its
laws and forces, implying that everything is God—or
pieces of Him, such as the stars, sun, moon, earth, you,
your cat, and even its fleas—ad infinitum. Consequently,
since He is evident in nature, there's no need for a
supernatural explanation of His existence. All of which
coincides with the doctrine of naturalism, as well as with
secular humanism, and its spiritual counterpart, New
Ageism.

But what does pantheism have to do with collectivism? Well, in itself, pantheism is collectivism—metaphysi-
cally that is, since, collectively, man has been deified,
making us all one. Thus glorifying us as a whole, or
collective, having defined away its parts, and individuality.
Oh, and even our consciousness, deeming it but part of a
greater (or collective) one, perhaps God's. As Texe Marrs
notes: "Man, the New Agers believe, is both a piece of the
whole and the whole itself." Then, quoting New Age
author Ruth Montgomery (or what her spirit guides said),
he adds: "We are as much God as God is a part of
us . . . each of us is God . . . together we are God . . . this
all-for-one-and-one-for-all . . . makes us the whole of
God."[31]

Even believing this is to be collectivized, and being
collectivized is to be ant-like, tractable, and dependent,
with a communal or "all-for-one-and-one-for-all" mentality, which logically, leads to political collectivism: ownership and control of everything by the people collectively.
While actually "the people," individually or collectively,
own and control nothing, not even themselves, being but

ants—wingless workers, unable to fly over the communal, underground cuckoo's nest. Or what Marx (and Lenin) falsely called the "dictatorship of the proletariat."

Still, this doesn't mean that everyone who promotes collectivism, or a Socialist super-state, is pantheistic. One may simply believe that the world is like a fragile spaceship in need of repair; and that, since we're all in it together, any effort to save it should be a collective one, such as through the UN (or a world government). Especially if, as perceived, the spaceship's problems are environmental, including having too many passengers, and not enough resources for them.

Even the behavior of the passengers may be a problem. Particularly when it obstructs spaceship solidarity, as in the case of certain Christians, for example, who are too exclusive, even intolerant, which, it is said, leads to inhumanity, as well as disunity. So the only solution is the "new humanism which embraces all people."[32] That is, an official, humanistic world religion, which itself is exclusive and intolerant, disallowing beliefs it hasn't sanctioned.

Many who promote this "new humanism" (or world religion) profess to be Christians themselves, and they are usually associated with the National/World Council of Churches (NCC/WCC). This makes them part of the solidarity revolution, knowingly or not, being but suctorial organs on the milli-UNopus' tentacles, oozing and twitching in response to the Rocky-Bye-implanted microchip in its brain, while imagining this has something to do with the kingdom of God and, of course, world peace.

Actually, Rocky-Bye doesn't care what we think so long as we "think globally," even if we don't know why. Since then we'd at least be unobstructive, while mindlessly promoting its revolution, being uncritical of its ends, or even receptive to them. Obliviously, like ants with diminutive, primatial brains, semi-consciously committed to their communal interests. Whatever they may be.

Basically, people haven't changed since Weishaupt's time, for they still "think" without actually thinking which is why Rocky-Bye's propagandizing (via its solidarity revolution) is so effective, especially in providing reasons for "thinking globally." Such as in its Club of Rome report:

> We must act locally but think globally. Whether we like it or not, we cannot act just locally. Whatever we do in one place and one time inevitably has repercussions in other places and other times. Even relatively minor and seemingly personal choices, such as those associated with lifestyles, dietary preferences, and preferred forms of transportation, have global impact when multiplied by the numbers of people in relatively prosperous societies. And even the private choices of career and family size make a difference to patterns of development and well-being in poor and rich countries alike.
>
> Hence global goals are goals for everyone. They need to be present in the planning of powerful governmental leaders as well as in the thinking of ordinary people. . . . If we [ignore the global], we shall collectively generate conditions that will depress the quality, and even the bare chances, of life on our planet.[33]

Yet, there's a class of people who are somewhat ignored, even though they don't "think globally," since they don't even think—but feel instead. In the sense that they're preoccupied with their immediate "needs," as they imagine them to be, which, generally, relate to sex, drugs, alcohol, food, entertainment, relaxation, and, of course, money for obtaining them. As a result, they tend to be amoral, irreligious, and apolitical, usually drifting with the current, and are therefore trendy, easily influenced—and led. Orwell calls them the "proles":

> [The] Party taught that the proles were natural inferiors who must be kept in subjection, like animals, by the application of a few simple rules. . . . So long as they continued to work and breed, their other activities were without importance. . . . [Such as,] care of home and children, petty quarrels with neighbors, films, football, beer, and above all, gambling. . . . It was not desirable that the proles should have strong political feelings. All that was required of them was a primitive patriotism which could be appealed to [in order to manipulate them]. And even when they became discontented, [it] led nowhere, because . . . they could only focus it on petty . . . grievances. The larger evils invariably escaped their notice.[34]

However, Orwell's proles are somewhat different than today's, especially in America where, generally, they're the dumbed-down (and hung-up) products of a sham public school system, and politically-correct educated illiterates of higher pseudoeducation. Mental paraplegics with sitcom norms, whose loony-tune worldviews are further being distorted by Rocky-Bye's "Ministry of Truth," particularly its CFR-controlled national media (TV, radio, press) wherein CFR members serve as propagandists. Some examples are: Brinkley, Sawyer, Walters (ABC-TV); Rather, Holland, (CBS-TV); Ferraro, Jackson, Kalb (CNN-TV); Brokaw (NBC-TV); Buckley, Hunter-Gault, Geyer (PBS-TV). Others serve with, to name a few: American Journal (radio), Associated Press, *Atlantic Monthly, Business Week, Forbes, Fortune, LA Times, Money, National Review, NY Times, Newsweek, Parade, Time, U.S. News & World Report, Wall Street Journal, Washington Post.*[35]

Rocky-Bye-Baby (including its "Ministry of Truth") cannot, of course, explicitly describe its conspiratorial designs (i.e., plans, objectives), since, by definition, they're illegal. It can, though, say that it wants world government, a new order, etc., provided it doesn't say why—truthfully, that is. It must sugar-coat itself with altruism, falsely, as in consciousness-raising (including the expansion of our "inner limits"), so that we can begin thinking—and acting—globally in the building of "a new world [wherein we can] live with more dignity and greater equality than ever before."[36]

But the proles don't understand this since, to them, Rocky-Bye doesn't exist, nor does its agenda. For it's never mentioned on the telly. And besides, they don't think, but feel instead, imagining that America is now "great again"—and that communism is dead. Sure, there's still problems—like inequality, crime, and pollution—but none our government can't solve. If only we'd give it more power.

Such is their mindset, or "feelset," and why Orwell called them "the dumb masses," which are about 85% of Oceania's population. The rest is its ruling class: Outer Party (13%) and the Inner Party (2%). Thus, being the majority, the proles were Winston's only hope—at first: "If there was hope, it must lie in the proles, because only there, in those swarming disregarded masses . . . could the force to destroy the Party ever be generated. . . . [If] only they could somehow become conscious of their own strength, [they] would have no need to conspire. They needed only to rise up and shake themselves like a horse shaking off flies. If they chose they could blow the Party to pieces. . . . Surely sooner or later it must occur to them to do it. And yet—!"[37]

Winston suddenly realized the proles would never rebel. Why not? Well, it's not their nature. They live in a little world—their only reality. Wherein, of course, their consciousness lies, hidden and impervious from without. As Winston somewhat implies, enigmatically: "Until they become conscious they will never rebel, and until after they have rebelled they cannot become conscious."[38]

Yet, they couldn't be made to rebel since the Party was all-powerful. Besides, they weren't fully conscious of being oppressed. For being unobstructive, the Party found them useful, giving them perhaps a false sense of security. As later confirmed by O'Brien: "The proletarians will never revolt, not in a thousand years. . . . They cannot. I do not have to tell you the reason; you know it already."[39]

Today's proles aren't rebelling (i.e., resisting tyranny) either, being oblivious to the new Oceania's near completion. That is, heedless of its many signs, they are unaware of its Orwellian potentials: social engineering, psycho-physical experimentation, and genocidal cleansing, all within a global society wherein (unlike Orwell's Oceania) they will be numbered, profiled, and kept under surveillance, with the use of microchips.

But actually we'll all be proles, being members of the lowest class, the non-ruling one—"in which [as workers we can] live with more dignity and greater equality than ever before in history," according to the Club.[40] Yet most members of the solidarity revolution will fare no better since, after "their" revolutionary end (i.e., world government) has been realized, they will no longer be useful, being, in a sense, the means to that end and thus justifiably dispensable, contrary to their expectations.

Many, if not most, of the high-level positions will go to today's Communist officials. As those in the Soviet Union, Communist China, Vietnam, N. Korea, and Cuba. Countries that will, in a sense, be the new Oceania, which (like Orwell's Oceania) would be collectivistic, since the "free" world countries will have been assimilated. A process during which many of us will be extremely vulnerable, especially Christians and patriots, and those in the fields of government, business, and education.[41]

Our vulnerability will also be determined by our thinking, since, as in Oceania, all thinking must be politically correct. And any thought that isn't will be a "crime," or what Orwell calls a "thoughtcrime"—"the essential crime that [contains] all others in itself," which, says Winston, "was not a thing that could be concealed forever.

[For] sooner or later [the Thought Police] were bound to get you." He adds: "It was always at night—the arrests invariably happened at night. The sudden jerk out of sleep, the rough hand shaking your shoulder, the lights glaring in your eyes, the ring of hard faces round the bed. In the vast majority of cases there was no trial, no report of the arrest. People simply disappeared, always during the night."[42]

Of course, thoughts would not be "crimes" until they were expressed, detected, or imagined; and, in the new Oceania, they would take many forms, verbal and nonverbal. Whatever is imaginable, or even unimaginable, such as having no form at all, like doing nothing—including, ironically, thinking nothing, since even a thoughtless facial expression (suggesting one's thoughts are being concealed) would be a crime—one Orwell calls a "facecrime": "The smallest thing could give you . . . away. A nervous tic, an unconscious look of anxiety, a habit of muttering to yourself—anything that carried with it the suggestion of abnormality, of having something to hide. In any case, to wear an improper expression on your face . . . was itself a punishable offense."[43]

In the new Oceania, everything would be a "punishable offense," even emotions, but particularly anger and its many petty, related forms, since (through re-definition) it could be equated with hatred and called a "hate crime," even though hatred is a mental-emotional condition, rather than an act arising from it. Logically enough. To "the Party" though, truth and logic would be but obstacles to its exercise of power and control. For, as in Oceania, power would be an end, "not a means." As O'Brien explains to Winston: "The Party seeks power entirely for its own sake. We are not interested in the good of others; we are interested solely in power. . . . We are different from all the oligarchies of the past in that we know what we are doing. . . . We know that no one ever seizes power with the intention of relinquishing it. Power is not a means; it is an end. One does not establish a dictatorship in order to safeguard a revolution; one makes the revolution in order to establish the dictatorship."[44]

So, in the new Oceania, it will be impossible not to commit a crime, and also impossible to hide it, since everyone will be spying on each other, especially children. For, as in the Soviet Union and Nazi Germany, they'll be organized and trained for this very purpose—to spy on parents, neighbors, teachers, etc., and to do so with impunity, thus making them loathsome and unbearable. As in Oceania: "[By] means of such organizations as the Spies they were systematically turned into ungovernable little savages, [except for not wanting] to rebel against the discipline of the Party. . . . [So it] was almost normal for people . . . to be frightened of their own children. [Who often] denounced [them] to the Thought Police."[45]

Even ordinary activities will be criminalized (e.g., correcting your children, holding a prayer meeting, walking in the woods), especially if they can be associated with abuse, drugs, sedition, terrorism, and the environment. For rather than to maintain order, the purpose of the new Oceania's "Ministry of Love" will be to create disorder. Why? Several reasons: (1) So "the Party" can control and manipulate the people; (2) exercise and expand its power; (3) justify its existence; (4) and sustain itself.

But there's much more to it than that. Since (we are to believe) there would be "world peace," and thus no more war, which, according to Rocky-Bye, is needed "for stabilizing and controlling national economies."[46] So, without war, there would have to be warless—uh, peaceful wars, or, at least, "a substitute for [them]." One "that would provide the same 'stabilizing' function,"[47] like fighting environmental crime, which could easily be fabricated. There would, of course, be other crimes too, particularly those requiring "Operations Other Than War (OOTW),"[48] including "peacekeeping."

"World peace" then would not be peace at all. Except as redefined, meaning that all resistance to communism will have ceased,[49] on the national level, that is. Since, except for the new Oceania, there would be no more nations. So rather than war, there'd be "peace-keeping," or "peaceful" wars; and we, the people, would be the enemy, collectively, about four billion of us—before the "cleansing"—all subject to the whims of Allen's "power-seeking [multi]billionaires,"[50] possibly ten,[51] one being dominant and, perhaps, more evil, whom we can call "Big Brother," the "guise in which the Party [would choose] to exhibit itself to the world. His function [being]," writes Orwell, "to act as a focusing point for love, fear, and reverence, emotions which are more easily felt toward an individual than toward an organization."[52]

The new Oceania then would be the most comprehensive, and bizarre, social order known to man. Wherein billions, of all races, would be enslaved by a tiny circle of elite, super-rich Caucasians. Of course, as these elitists describe it, it would be a "qualitatively new world order"[53] in which, we are assured, "all people could live with more dignity and greater equality than ever before."[54] Even though, as they admit, this new order would include the Communist states, wherein there is no dignity, and equality means being equally, or collectively, oppressed. Why? Because they're Oceanias, awaiting the "Great Merger,"[55] their ultimate transformation, or consolidation into Allen's "all-powerful world socialist super-state,"[56] the new Oceania. Where, as in Orwell's Oceania, there "will be no love, except the love of Big Brother," and "no laughter, except the laugh of triumph over [the] enemy." Us. "But always," says O'Brien to Winston

> . . . there will be the intoxication of power, constantly increasing and constantly growing subtler. Always, at every moment, there will be the thrill of victory, the sensation of trampling on an enemy [i.e., us] who is helpless. If you want a picture of the future, imagine a boot stamping on a human face—forever.[57]

Notes

Chapter One—Rocky-Bye-Baby

1. R. Emmett Tyrrell, Jr., *The Liberal Crack-Up*, Simon & Schuster, New York, 1984, pp. 26-27.

2. In *The Shadows of Power* (Western Islands, Boston, 1988, p. 154), James Perloff writes: "With [Gary Allen's] *None Dare Call It Conspiracy* putting the heat on the CFR, David Rockefeller moved to form a new internationalist organization—the Trilateral Commission. For some three decades, CFR members had pushed for 'Atlantic Union,' a bilateral federation of America and Europe. The [TC] broadened this objective to include an Asiatic leg. . . . Helping [Rockefeller] develop the concept was Zbigniew Brzezinski. . . ."

3. Barry M. Goldwater, *With No Apologies*, William Morrow & Co., New York, 1979, p. 287.

4. Gary Allen, "Regan at Treasury," *American Opinion*, February 1981, p. 25.

5. Ibid., p. 18.

6. Gary Allen, "The Republican Convention and Ronald Reagan," *American Opinion*, September 1980, p. 99.

7. Note 3, p. 284.

8. Ibid., p. 285.

9. Kitty Kelley, *Nancy Reagan*, Pocket/Simon & Schuster, New York, 1991, p. 426.

10. Antony C. Sutton, *Two Faces of George Bush*, CPA Book Publisher, P.O. Box 596, Boring, OR, 1988, p. 81.

11. Paul M. Weyrich, "The White House, The 1982 Elections, And The Right," *American Opinion*, April 1982, p. 10.

12. Anonymous.

13. Note 6, p. 100.

14. Ibid., p. 109.

15. Gary Allen, *Say "No!" to the New World Order*, Concord Press, Seal Beach, CA, 1987, p. 95.

16. Gary Allen with Larry Abraham, *None Dare Call It Conspiracy*, Concord Press, Seal Beach, CA, 1971, p. 130.

17. Paul M. Weyrich, "What Leadership Is And What It Is Not," *Conservative Digest*, March 1987, p. 39.

18. Paul M. Weyrich, "We Can Win If We Stop Being Jerks," *Conservative Digest*, October 1987, p. 17.

19. Ibid., p. 21.

20. Ron Paul, "Strengthening the Chains of the Constitution," *The New American*, 16 February 1987, p. 53.

21. Joel Bainerman, *The Crimes of a President*, S.P.I. Books/Shapolsky Publishers, Inc., New York, 1992, pp. 10-13.

22. John F. McManus, "Will-of-the-Wisp," *The New American*, 9 November 1987, p. 17.

23. Note 9, p. 310.

24. Ibid., p. 311.

25. Ibid., p. 507.

26. Ibid., p. 539.

27. Ibid., pp. 373-374.

28. Ibid., p. 419.

29. Jeanne Wright and Pat Hilton, "Snooping around 668 St. Cloud," *USA Weekend*, 23-25 June 1989, p. 5.

30. "The New World Order in Control," The American Freedom Movement newsletter, March 1989, p. 2.

31. "Did You Know?" The John Birch Society *Bulletin*, May 1989, p. 28.

32. "Find Out About This New Commission!" The American Freedom Movement newsletter, March 1988, p. 9.

33. *The Fact Finder*, Scottsdale, AZ, 1 September 1994, p. 1.

34. "Australia," The American Freedom Movement newsletter, March 1988, p. 8.

35. "More U.S. Money to Communists," The American Freedom Movement newsletter, October 1988, p. 10.

36. "Kissinger," The American Freedom Movement newsletter, June 1989, p. 7.

37. Council on Foreign Relations, *Annual Report 1985-1986*, 58 East 68th Street, New York, NY 10021, p. 96.

38. Kirk Kidwell, "The Triumph of the Insiders," *The New American*, 13 February 1989, p. 9.

39. Gary Allen, *Kissinger*, '76 Press, Seal Beach, CA, 1976, pp. 25-26.

40. Note 37, p. 31.

41. John F. McManus, "Nothing Else Makes Any Sense," *The New American*, 13 March 1989, p. 25.

42. Note 37, p. 50.

43. Texe Marrs, *Dark Majesty*, Living Truth Publishers, Austin, TX, 1992, p. 105.

44. Note 37, p. 90.

45. Larry Abraham, *Call It Conspiracy*, Double A Publications, Seattle, 1985, p. 196.

46. A. Ralph Epperson, *The Unseen Hand*, Publius Press, Tucson, 1985, p. 415.

47. " 'George and David' or Should It Be 'David and George,' " The American Freedom Movement newsletter, April 1989, p. 6.

48. Alan Stang, "What the Trilateralists Want From You," *American Opinion*, May 1980, p. 104.

49. Note 46, p. 236.

50. Zbigniew Brzezinski, *Between Two Ages*, Viking Press, New York, 1970, pp. 308-309.

51. *Who's Who in America*, 44 Edition 1986-1987, Vol. 1, pp. 376-377.

52. Note 50, p. 258.

53. Ibid., pp. 271-272.

54. Ibid., pp. 258-259.

55. Note 38, p. 9.

56. Gary Benoit, "Reagan vs. Reagan," *The New American*, 23 May 1988, p. 28.

57. Warren P. Mass, "Alabama's Daring Defense," *The New American*, 23 May 1988, p. 21.

58. Dr. Charles A. Provan, The American Freedom Movement newsletter, August 1988, p. 3.

59. Ibid.

60. Note 47.

61. Note 38, p. 7.

62. James J. Drummey, "Bush and the USSR," *The New American*, 19 June 1989, p. 11.

63. *The Merriam-Webster Dictionary*, 1974 ed.

64. Ervin Laszlo, et al., *Goals for Mankind*, 1977; Signet, New York, 1978, p. 52.

65. David B. Funderburk, *Betrayal of America*, Box 1124, Dunn, NC 28334, 1991, p. 61.

66. The John Birch Society *Bulletin*, February 1987, p. 15.

67. Ibid.

68. *Congressional Record*, 15 December 1987, pp. S18145-S18150.

69. Texe Marrs, *Millenium*, Living Truth Publishers, Austin, TX, 1990, pp. 109-111.

70. James J. Drummey, "Wide Gulf Remains After Summit," *The New American*, 9 December 1985, p. 24.

71. William F. Jasper, "Sovietizing America's Children," The John Birch Society *Bulletin*, June 1988, pp. 4-5.

72. "U.S.-Soviet Contacts Expand in Wake of Summit," *Human Events*, 10 May 1986, p. 3.

73. "Preliminaries to the Summit," *The New American*, 25 November 1985, p. 9.

74. W. Cleon Skouson, *The Naked Capitalist*, Skouson, Salt Lake City, 1970, pp. 108-109.

75. Rael Jean Isaac and Erich Isaac, *The Coercive Utopians*, Regnery Gateway, Chicago, 1983, p. 116.

76. Note 72.

77. *Freedom From War*, Department of State Publication 7277, Washington, September 1961, p. 19.

78. W. L. Fieldhouse, "The War on Gun Ownership Still Goes On," *Guns & Ammo*, February 1992, p. 20.

79. *The World Almanac*, 1989, p. 37.

80. Jane H. Ingraham, "The Fall of Nicaragua," *The New American*, 17 July 1989, p. 26.

81. Antony C. Sutton, *The Best Enemy Money Can Buy*, Liberty House Press, Billings, MT, 1986.

82. Note 62.

83. Note 80, pp. 26-27.

84. Note 21, p. 108.

85. "Conservatives Battle South African Policy," *Human Events*, 28 September 1985, pp. 3-4.

86. Note 56, p. 32. (Re: Presidential Determination 82-19)

87. Ibid. (Re: Presidential Determination 84-11)

88. Note 64.

89. *The World Almanac*, 1992, p. 516.

90. Ibid., p. 437.

91. James Perloff, *The Shadows of Power*, Western Islands, Boston, 1988, p. 172.

92. Note 89, back cover.

93. Note 79, p. 438.

94. "What Really Happened to KAL 007?" *The Alan Stang Radio Report*, Los Angeles, 7 November 1985. Also *The New American*, 29 August 1988, pp. 25-37.

95. Avraham Shifrin, press release (Research Centre, Jerusalem), 11 July 1991; The American Freedom Movement newsletter, November 1991, pp. 1-8.

96. Susan L. M. Huck, "Founding of the Society," *American Opinion,* March 1985, p. 140.

97. Warren P. Mass, "Kathryn McDonald's Crusade," *The New American,* 29 August 1988, p. 18.

98. Lawrence T. Patterson, *A Monthly Lesson in Criminal Politics* (P.O. Box 37432, Cincinnati, OH 45222) newsletter, 28 February 1987, p. 14.

99. Note 73.

100. Note 56, p. 33.

101. Robert W. Lee, "World Court and Genocide," *American Opinion,* February 1985, p. 23.

102. Note 29.

103. Note 68.

104. Note 9, p. 528.

105. Dr. Charles A. Provan, The American Freedom Movement newsletter, February 1988, p. 6.

106. George J. Church, "A Gentle Battle of Images," *Time,* 13 June 1988, p. 22.

107. Note 16.

108. Note 9, p. 67.

109. Ron Matheson, "Conservatives eye action plan for '95," *The National Educator,* December 1994, p. 11.

110. "Reagan's Stunning 'Volte Face' on the USSR," *Human Events,* 19 December 1987, p. 3.

111. Ibid., p. 4.

112. Ibid.

113. Note 64.

114. Note 65.

115. Ibid.

116. Note 68.

117. Note 66.

118. Note 47.

119. Martin Anderson, *Revolution,* Harcourt Brace Jovanovich, New York, 1988, p. 313.

120. Council on Foreign Relations, *Annual Report 1987-1988,* New York, p. 107.

121. Note 9, p. 310.

122. Note 10, p. 81.

123. Note 21, p. 35.

124. Note 119, p. 289.

125. Ibid., p. 292.

126. Ibid. (Also see p. 291. Actually Reagan wasn't "helpless." He simply allowed his staff to run the show; and, if he had to "rely on what [was] or [was] not brought to him," it was because "he [did] not . . . search out and demand things." Which means "disaster [was invited to] strike.")

127. Ibid., pp. 306-321.

128. Ibid., pp. 317-318.

129. Ibid., pp. 222-234.

130. Note 9, p. 423.

131. Michael K. Deaver, *Behind the Scenes,* William Morrow, New York, 1987, p. 35.

132. Note 9, p. iii.

133. Note 131, pp. 82-83.

134. Mark D. Isaacs, "God Save Us from Activist Presidents!" *The New American,* 4 July 1988, p. 53.

135. Ronald Reagan, *Ronald Reagan's Own Story,* 1965; Karz-Segil, New York, 1981, p. 105.

Chapter Two—Peace, Peace, Peace

1. Ronald Reagan, *Ronald Reagan's Own Story,* 1965; Karz-Segil, New York, 1981, p. 33.

2. Ibid., p. 23.

3. Harold Adams, *The History of Eureka College*, Board of Trustees of Eureka College, Eureka, IL, p. 14.

4. Ibid., p. 266.

5. "Ronald Reagan—Class of 1932," Eureka College brochure.

6. Note 1, p. 23.

7. Note 3, p. 79.

8. Note 5.

9. Note 3, p. 260.

10. "Eureka College president to resign," *Woodford Reporter*, 13 February 1985, p. 1.

11. *Eureka College Catalog 1984-85*, p. 27.

12. Ibid., p. 10.

13. Allen Fore, "An Interview With President Dan Gilbert," *The Pegasus* (Eureka College student newspaper), 17 February 1984, p. 11.

14. Anonymous. (Interview with faculty member.)

15. Note 3, p. 11.

16. Eureka Christian Church 1983-84 *Yearbook*, p. 29.

17. Rael Jean Isaac and Erich Isaac, *The Coercive Utopians*, Regnery Gateway, Chicago, 1983, pp. 162-163.

18. Note 3, p. 309.

19. Note 11, p. 107.

20. Keith E. Clark, "Local Action," *The Disciple*, January 1986, p. 19.

21. Note 3, p. 309.

22. Note 16.

23. James L. Merrell, ed., "Viewpoint," *The Disciple*, 6 November 1983, p. 5.

24. Bob Slosser, *Reagan Inside Out*, Word Books, Waco, TX, 1984, p. 36.

25. Kitty Kelley, *Nancy Reagan,* Pocket/Simon & Schuster, New York, 1991, p. 109.

26. Ibid., p. 85.

27. Note 1, p. 233.

28. Keith E. Clark, "A Man Who Played God," *The Disciple,* 6 November 1983, pp. 14-15.

29. Ibid.

30. Ibid.

31. Herbert Schlossberg, *Idols for Destruction,* Thomas Nelson, Nashville, 1983, pp. 265-266.

32. Ibid., p. 266.

33. Ephesians 6:12.

34. Randall N. Baer, *Inside the New Age Nightmare,* Huntington House, Lafayette, LA, 1989, p. 84.

35. Eugene W. Brice, "A Disciple by Choice," *The Disciple,* 6 November 1983, p. 17.

36. Robert K. Welsh, *Characteristic Beliefs of the Christian Church* brochure, Christian Board of Publications, St. Louis, no date, pp. 6-7.

37. Richard L. Harrison, *Our History* brochure, Christian Board of Publications, St. Louis, no date, p. 2.

38. C. Roy Stouffer, "Since You Asked," *The Disciple,* January 1986, p. 58.

39. Revelation 20:1-6.

40. Johanna Newman, "Leaders get along like old friends," *USA Today,* 9 December 1987, p. A-6.

41. Note 36, p. 6.

42. Ibid., pp. 6-7.

43. Kirk Kidwell, "UN Has Noble Purposes?" *The New American,* 13 October 1986, p. 22.

44. Texe Marrs, *Mystery Mark of the New Age,* Crossway Books, Westchester, IL, 1988, p. 102.

45. Robert W. Lee, *The United Nations Conspiracy*, Western Islands, Boston, 1981, p. 20.

46. John F. McManus, "Reagan Wrong About UN," *The New American*, 27 October 1986, p. 22.

47. Donald T. Regan, "For the Record," *Time*, 16 May 1988, p. 26.

48. Joyce Wadler, et al., "The President's Astrologers," *People*, 23 May 1988, p. 108.

49. Note 25, p. 147.

50. Ibid., p. 164.

51. Ibid., p. 165.

52. Deuteronomy 18: 10-12.

53. Note 25, p. 110.

54. Note 44, p. 66.

55. Ibid., p. 67.

56. Texe Marrs, *Dark Majesty*, Living Truth Publishers, Austin, 1992, p. 27.

57. Cathy Burns, *Hidden Secrets of Masonry*, Sharing, 212 E. 7th Street, Mt. Carmel, PA, 17851-2211, p. 36.

58. Note 34, p. 99.

59. Note 25, pp. 80-81.

60. Joseph J. Carr, *The Twisted Cross*, Huntington House, Shreveport, LA, 1985, p. 277.

61. Note 17, p. 270.

62. Ibid., p. 269.

63. Note 1, pp. 164-165.

64. Ibid., p. 141.

65. Ibid., pp. 233-234.

66. *People*, May 1985, p. 138.

67. Michael K. Deaver, *Behind the Scenes*, William Morrow, New York, 1987, p. 226.

68. Ibid., p. 111.

69. Note 25, pp. 479-480.

70. Note 67, p. 39.

71. Ibid., pp. 103-104.

72. "How Key Reagan Aide Did in Conservatives," *Human Events*, 28 November 1987, p. 3.

73. Note 67, pp. 103-104.

74. Note 1, pp. 138-139.

75. Ibid., p. 139.

76. Ibid., p. 141.

77. Ibid., p. 140.

78. Ibid., p. 141.

79. Ibid., p. 165.

80. Gary Allen, *Say "No!" to the New World Order*, Concord Press, Seal Beach, CA, 1987, p. 53.

81. Letter dated 16 October 1985 from Ronald Reagan to Senator Robert J. Dole.

82. Peter Lalonde, "Genocide Treaty—a globalist tool, *Christian Inquirer*, April 1985, p. 26.

83. Note 45, p. 142.

84. Note 80, pp. 53-54.

85. "Disciples Comment on WCC Conference," *The Disciple*, 19 October 1980, p. 24.

86. Note 43.

87. Ervin Laszlo, et al., *Goals for Mankind*, 1977; Signet, New York, 1978, p. 310.

88. Ibid., p. 350.

89. Ibid., p. 338.

90. Ibid., p. 52.

91. Marian Leighton, "The Soviets, the Pope and 'Liberation Theology,'" *Human Events*, 23 March 1985, p. 12.

92. News Briefs, *The Disciple*, January 1986, pp. 32-33.

93. James R. Ryan, "Getting Started," *The Disciple*, January 1986, pp. 20-21.

94. News agency releases as found in numerous publications (e.g., *The State Journal*, Frankfort, KY).

95. "News from the Nation's Capital," *The New American*, 2 December 1985, p. 12; James J. Drummey, "Wide Gulf Remains After Summit," *The New American*, 9 December 1985, p. 24.

96. Note 94.

Chapter Three—And More Peace

1. Keith E. Clark, "Local Action," *The Disciple*, January 1986, p. 18.

2. "Ecumenical partnership celebrates differences," *The Disciple*, August 1986, p. 30.

3. Rael Jean Isaac and Erich Isaac, *The Coercive Utopians*, Regnery Gateway, Chicago, 1983, p. 32.

4. Mary O'Brien, "Chavis Lecture," *The Pegasus*, 28 November 1983, p. 1.

5. Art Andrews, "Canceled Falwell speech arouses Eureka students," *The Journal Star*, Peoria, 5 September 1985, p. 1, Sec. C.

6. "Dare to Oppose Worship of a Nation-State," Evening Vesper program, Eureka College, 29 November 1983.

7. Letters to the Editor, *Woodford County Journal*, 2 February 1984, p. 5.

8. Letter to the Editor, *Woodford County Journal*, 19 January 1984.

9. Note 7, p. 6.

10. "$500,000 Pledge Made to Reagan Program," *News and Ideas* (Eureka College newsletter), March 1984, p. 2.

11. "America returning to basic values, President says," *Woodford County Journal*, 9 February 1984.

12. Kim Perz, "Reagan Recaps 50 Years of Transition in America," *The Pegasus*, 17 February 1984, p. 1.

13. "What's the dove all about?" Focus (Eureka College student organization) announcement, 8 February 1984.

14. Illinois Valley Broadcasting Corporation brochure, January 1984.

15. Ibid., preliminary draft.

16. Ibid.

17. Note 3, p. 156.

18. Louise Rees, "Names And Covert Operations Of Those K.G.B. Spies At The U.N." *American Opinion*, April 1985, p. 83.

19. Note 3, p. 116.

20. Marian Leighton, "The Soviets, the Pope and 'Liberation Theology,'" *Human Events*, 23 March 1985, p. 12.

21. Note 3, p. 195.

22. Ibid., p. 156.

23. Note 18, p. 89.

24. Note 3, p. 122.

25. "Defense, faith wrestle on ways to avoid war," *The Disciple*, 6 November 1983, p. 23.

26. James D. Bales, *The Phoenix Papers: If Not Treason, What?* Christian Crusade Publications, Box 977, Tulsa 2, OK, 1966, p. 5.

27. Note 3, p. 123.

28. Roger Miller, "Speakers address apartheid problem," *The Pegasus*, 26 April 1985, p. 1.

29. Jane Nohl, "Coalition asks for state divestment from South Africa," *Woodford County Journal*, 2 May 1985, p. 5.

30. Rev. Gary M. Hedrick, letter to Rev. Glenn E. Riddell, Jr., Eureka College, 10 May 1985.

31. Kirk Kidwell, "The African National Congress Sets Its Sights on South Africa," *The New American*, 14 October 1985, p. 5.

Chapter Four—Blood, Bones, and the Kingdom of God

1. John O. Humbert, "From the General Minister and President," *The Disciple*, May 1986, p. 60.

2. D. Scarborough, ed., Gospel Defence League (P.O. Box 17007, 1061 Regent road, 8000 Cape Town, R.S.A.), newsletter, February 1986, p. 1. Their source: Ecumenical Press Service (World Council of Churches), 16-31 December 1985.

3. Note 1.

4. Note 2.

5. "The Kairos Document," *Signposts* (Signpost Publications and Research Centre, P.O. Box 26148, Arcadia 0007, South Africa), Vol. 5, No. 6, 1986, p. 6.

6. Gospel Defence League newsletter, December 1985, p. 2.

7. Paul Johnson, *Modern Times*, Harper & Row, New York, 1983, pp. 412-413.

8. Note 1.

9. Henry W. Bragdon and Samuel P. McCutchen, *History of a Free People*, 1954; Macmillan, New York, 1961, p. 41.

10. James L. Merrell, "Viewpoint: Faithful biblical proclamation still turns the world upside down," *The Disciple*, June 1986, p. 5.

11. Ibid.

12. The Gospel Defence League, *The Archbishop and The Bible* (booklet), passim.

13. Ibid.

14. Richard Wurmbrand, *Marx & Satan*, Crossway Books, Westchester, IL, 1986, pp. 125-126.

15. Dr. T. Hugh Moreton and Rev. N. W. Hutchings, *World Council of Churches*, Southwest Radio Church, P.O. Box 1144, Oklahoma City, OK 73101, p. 38.

16. David P. Gaines, *The World Council of Churches*, The Richard R. Smith Co., Inc., Peterborough, NH, 1966, pp. 36-37.

17. Gary Allen, *Say "No!" to the New World Order,* Concord Press, Seal Beach, CA, 1987, p. 189.

18. Ervin Laszlo, et al., *Goals for Mankind,* 1977; Signet, New York, 1978, pp. 351-353.

19. Ibid., p. 299.

20. Note 12, p. 8.

21. Note 17, p. 190.

22. "June 16 Set as Day of Prayer and Fasting," *The Disciple,* June 1986, p. 15.

23. Donald S. McAlvany, "The African National Congress," *The New American,* 25 August 1986, pp. 23-24.

24. Warren L. McFerran, "A Meeting of Minds," *The New American,* 2 March 1987, p. 8.

25. Fr. James Thornton, "Recalling a Proud Past," *The New American,* 30 may 1994, p. 23.

26. Note 24, p. 9.

27. Note 23, p. 24.

28. Note 24, p. 10.

29. Gary Allen with Larry Abraham, *None Dare Call It Conspiracy,* Concord Press, Seal Beach, CA, 1971, p. 35.

30. Note 24, p. 11.

31. "An Open Letter to P. W. Botha," *The McAlvany Intelligence Advisor* (P.O. Box 39810, Phoenix, AZ 85069), October 1986, pp. 1-2.

32. "America in Decline: Betrayals, Bombs and Bankruptcies," *The McAlvany Intelligence Advisor* (newsletter), p. 7.

33. Jeane J. Kirkpatrick, *Dictatorships and Double Standards,* Simon & Schuster, New York, 1982, p. 23.

34. Ibid., p. 35.

35. Zbigniew Brzezinski, *Between Two Ages,* Viking Press, New York, 1970, p. 295.

36. Note 34.

37. Note 33, pp. 58-60.

38. James J. Drummey, "Gorbachev's View of History," *The New American*, 23 November 1987, p. 9.

39. Note 35, p. 83.

40. Ibid., p. 73.

41. Ibid., p. 74.

42. Ibid., p. 80.

43. Ibid., p. 74. Also see p. 123. As to these "perspectives and . . . concerns," Brzezinski writes: "[Marxism gave us] insight into contemporary reality; . . . infused political action with strong ethical elements; [made possible] a sustained attack on antiquated preindustrial social institutions; and . . . raised the banner of internationalism. . . ." Thus his "brave new world" would be a Marxist one wherein true Christianity would be nonexistent, since Marxism itself is a religion. Moreover, says Rev. Richard Wurmbrand (*Marx and Satan*, p. 81), "Satan is . . . its god."

44. Ibid.

45. Ibid.

46. Ibid., p. 75.

47. Ibid., p. 83.

48. Ibid., p. 92.

49. Ibid., p. 93.

50. Michael Voslensky, *Nomenklatura*, Doubleday, New York, 1984, p. 70.

51. Note 35, p. 64.

52. Ibid., p 65.

53. Ibid., p. 91.

54. Rev. Clarence Kelly, *Conspiracy Against God and Man*, Western Islands, Boston, 1974, p. 189.

55. Texe Marrs, *Dark Secrets of the New Age*, Crossway Books, Westchester, IL, 1987, p. 125.

56. Note 54 p. 191.

57. Ibid., p. 16.

58. Note 55, p. 127.

59. Ibid., p. 140.

60. Texe Marrs, *Mystery Mark of the New Age*, Crossway Books, Westchester, IL, 1988, p. 237.

61. Note 55, p. 134.

62. Note 17, p. 188.

63. Randall N. Baer, *Inside the New Age Nightmare*, Huntington House, Lafayette, LA, 1989, p. 84.

64. Paul Kurtz, ed., *Humanist Manifestos I and II*, 1973; Prometheus Books, Buffalo, 1984, p. 13.

65. Ibid., p. 21.

66. Note 63, p. 84.

67. Ibid., p. 85.

68. Ibid., pp. 166-167.

69. Note 55, pp. 204-228.

70. Ibid., pp. 49-55.

71. Note 60, p. 14.

72. Ibid., pp. 231-233.

73. Note 18, p. 360.

74. Ibid., p. 356.

75. Ibid., p. 301.

76. Ibid., p. 191.

Chapter Five—Another Dimension

1. Gary Allen with Larry Abraham, *None Dare Call It Conspiracy*, Concord Press, Seal Beach, CA, 1971, p. 35.

2. Herbert Schlossberg, *Idols for Destruction*, Thomas Nelson, Nashville, 1983, p. 253.

3. Ibid., pp. 332-333.

4. Gary Allen, *Say "No!" to the New World Order*, Concord Press, Seal Beach, CA, 1987, p. 188.

5. A. Ralph Epperson, *The Unseen Hand*, Publius Press, Tucson, 1985, p. 221.

6. Ibid..

7. Ibid., p. 222.

8. Texe Marrs, *New Age Cults & Religions*, Living Truth Ministries, Austin, 1990, p. 308.

9. Ibid., p. 88.

10. Dr. T. Hugh Moreton and Rev. N. W. Hutchings, *World Council of Churches*, Southwest Radio Church, Oklahoma City, 1983, p. 40.

11. Ibid., p. 3.

12. Ibid., p. 40.

13. David P. Gaines, *The World Council of Churches*, Noone House, Peterborough, NH, 1966, pp. 30-31.

14. Ibid., p. 31.

15. *The Encyclopaedia Britannica*, University Press, Cambridge, 1910, Vol 5, p. 858.

16. Carrol Quigley, *Tragedy & Hope*, Macmillan, New York, 1966, pp. 131-133. Also W. Cleon Skousen, *The Naked Capitalist*, Skousen, Salt Lake City, 1970, p. 30-31.

17. Ibid., Skousen, p. 38.

18. Note 13, p. 33.

19. Note 16, Skousen, pp. 29-30.

20. Note 13, p. 31.

21. Ibid., pp. 34-37.

22. Ibid., p. 37.

23. Ibid., p. 41.

24. Clarence B. Carson, *The Growth of America 1878-1928*, American Textbook Committee, Wadley, AL, 1985, Vol. 4, p. 49.

25. Note 15, p. 364.

26. Note 1, p. 62.

27. Ibid., p. 88.

28. Note 13, pp. 38-39.

29. Council on Foreign Relations, *Annual Report 1985-1986*, 58 East 68th St., New York, NY 10021, p. 64.

30. Henry W. Bragdon and Samuel P. McCutchen, *History of a Free People*, 1954; Macmillan, New York, 1961, p. 389.

31. Ibid., p. 556.

32. Paul Johnson, *Modern Times*, Harper & Row, New York, 1983, pp. 30-31.

33. Note 30, p. 542.

34. Note 5, p. 262.

35. Note 16, Skousen, p. 22. Also Quigley, p. 324.

36. Note 30, p. 539.

37. Note 1, p. 81.

38. Note 13, p. 38.

39. Note 16, Skousen, p. 33. Also Quigley, p. 951.

40. Ibid., Skousen, p. 34. Also Quigley, pp. 951-952.

41. Ibid., Skousen, pp. 23-24. Also Quigley, p. 122.

42. Note 1, p. 49.

43. Ibid., p. 65.

44. Ibid., p. 49 and p. 62.

45. Note 16, Skousen, p. 22. Also Quigley, p. 324.

46. Jane Ingraham, "The Horrors of House," *The New American*, 17 August 1987, pp. 41-42.

47. Alan Stang, "What The Trilateralists Want From You," *American Opinion*, May 1980, p. 9.

48. Robert W. Lee, *The United Nations Conspiracy*, Western Islands, Belmont, MA, 1981, p. 3.

49. Note 4, p. 41.

50. Ibid., p. 72.

51. Note 48, p. 5.

52. Note 4, p. 46.

53. Note 16, Skousen, p. 119.

54. Note 4, p. 44.

55. Ibid., pp. 49-50.

56. Note 48, pp. 141-142.

57. Note 1, p. 86.

58. Ibid., p. 35.

59. Note 4, p. 188.

60. William F. Jasper, *Global Tyranny . . . Step by Step*, Western Islands, Appleton, WI, 1992, p. 212.

61. *Prophecy Newsletter*, Vol. 1, No. 6, 1985, p. 6.

62. *Prophecy Newsletter*, Vol. 1, No. 8, 1985, p. 12.

63. Ibid.

64. Note 13, p. 213.

65. *The World Almanac and Book of Facts 1987*, p. 340.

66. Note 48, p. 141.

67. Ernest W. Lefever, *Amsterdam to Nairobi*, Ethics and Public Policy Center, Washington, 1979, pp. 8-9.

68. Ibid.

69. Ervin Laszlo, et al., *Goals for Mankind*, 1977; Signet, New York, 1978, p. 356.

70. Ibid., p. 191.

71. Ibid., p. 350.

72. Note 67, p. 59.

73. Note 69, p. 350.

74. Note 72, pp. 58-59.

75. Note 69, p. 151.

76. Note 67, p. 18.

77. Ibid., p. 28.

78. Note 1, p. 93.

79. Note 13, p. 231.

80. Ibid., pp. 253-254.

81. Note 4, p. 20.

82. Note 5, p. 221.

83. Note 67, p. 19.

84. Ibid., pp. 18-23.

85. Note 4, pp. 235-236.

86. Note 69, p. 151.

87. Note 67, p. 31.

88. Susan L. M. Huck, "The Council On Foreign Relations And The Senate," *American Opinion*, November 1979, p. 93.

89. Note 48, p. 245.

90. Note 5, p. 371.

91. Note 69, pp. 362-363.

92. Note 48, p. 20.

93. Note 13, pp. 648-650.

94. Note 69, pp. 309-310.

95. Ibid., p. 330.

96. Note 48, pp. 20-21.

97. Note 69, p. 328.

98. Ibid., p. 360.

99. Ibid., p. 360; p. 362.

100. Ibid., pp 328-330.

101. Lewis Carroll, *Alice's Adventures in Wonderland*, 1865; Penguin Books, New York, 1994, pp. 23-24.

Chapter Six—Solid-air-ity

1. Ervin Laszlo, et al., *Goals for Mankind*, 1977; Signet, New York, 1978, pp. xi-xii.

2. Ibid., p. 351.

3. Ibid.

4. Ibid., p. 350.

5. Ibid., p. 357.

6. Ibid., p. 360.

7. Ibid., p. 362.

8. Zbigniew Brzezinski, *Between Two Ages*, Viking Press, New York, 1970, p. 295.

9. The John Birch Society *Bulletin*, February 1987, p. 15.

10. David B. Funderburk, *Betrayal of America*, The Larry McDonald Foundation, P.O. Box 1124, Dunn, NC 28334, 1991, p. 61.

11. Texe Marrs, *Millennium*, Living Truth Ministries, Austin, 1990, pp. 109-110.

12. Note 1, pp. 50-51.

13. Ibid., p. 366.

14. Ibid., pp. xx-xxiv.

15. Gary H. Kah, *En Route to Global Occupation*, Huntington House, Lafayette, LA, 1992, p.85; p. 189.

16. *Aspen Institute for Humanistic Studies* (booklet), P.O. Box 222, Queenstown, MD 21658, March 1988.

17. William F. Jasper, *Global Tyranny . . . Step by Step*, Western Islands, Appleton, WI, 1992, p. 56.

18. Note 11, p. 44.

19. Ibid., p. 73.

20. Texe Marrs, *Dark Majesty*, Living Truth Publishers, Austin, 1992, p. 100.

21. Ibid., p. 161.

22. Ibid., p. 81.

23. Note 17, pp. 176-177.

24. Ibid., p. 224.

25. Note 20, p. 137.

26. Note 15, pp. 41-43.

27. Note 1, p. 366.

28. Gary Allen, *Say "No!" to the New World Order,* Concord Press, Seal Beach, CA, 1987, pp. 57-58.

29. Ibid.

30. Ibid.

31. Texe Marrs, *Flashpoint* (newsletter), Living Truth Ministries, Austin, September 1995, p. 1.

32. Note 28, pp. 57-58.

33. Note 1, p. i.

34. Ibid., p. 367.

35. Ibid., p. xvii.

36. Ibid., p. x.

37. Ibid., p. xi.

38. Ibid., p. 360.

39. Note 8, p. 9.

40. Ibid., p. 58.

41. Ibid., p. 61.

42. Ibid., p. 62.

43. Ibid., pp. 64-65.

44. Ibid., p. 272.

45. Ibid., p. 276.

46. Ibid., p. 273.

47. Ibid., p. 272.

48. Note 1, p. 362.

49. Ibid., p. 363.

50. Ibid., p. 362.

51. George Orwell, *1984,* Signet, New York, 1949; 1950, pp. 7-9.

52. Note 1, p. 362.

53. Ibid., p. 359.

54. Ibid., p. 336.

55. Note 51. pp. 171-175.

56. Ibid., p. 214.

57. Avraham Shifrin, *The First Guide Book to Prisons and Concentration Camps of the Soviet Union*, Bantam, New York, 1980, p. 42.

58. Michael Voslensky, *Nomenklatura*, Doubleday, New York, 1984, p. 280.

59. Note 51, p. 245.

60. Ibid., p. 170.

61. Ibid., p. 8.

62. Ibid., p. 205.

Chapter Seven—The New Oceania

1. Ervin Laszlo, et al., *Goals for Mankind*, 1977; Signet, New York, 1978, p. 360.

2. Ibid., p. 49.

3. Ibid., p. 360.

4. Ibid., p. 361.

5. Ibid., p. 362.

6. Ibid.

7. Ibid., p. 357.

8. Ibid., pp. 49-52.

9. Ibid., pp. 52-53.

10. Michael Voslensky, *Nomenklatura*, Doubleday, New York, 1984, p. 96.

11. Ibid., pp. 172-173.

12. Ibid., pp. 106-107.

13. Avraham Shifrin, *The First Guide Book to Prisons and Concentration Camps of the Soviet Union*, Bantam, New York, 1980, pp. 3-4.

14. Gary Allen with Larry Abraham, *None Dare Call It Conspiracy*, Concord Press, Seal Beach, CA, 1971, p. 35.

15. Note 1, p. 191.

16. Note 14.

17. Zbigniew Brzezinski, *Between Two Ages*, Viking Press, New York, 1970, p. 293.

18. Ibid., pp. 296-297.

19. Ibid., p. 78.

20. Ibid., p. 124.

21. Ibid., pp. 72-74.

22. Note 1, pp. 337-338.

23. Ibid., pp. 190-191.

24. Ibid., p. 151.

25. Department of State Publication 7277, *Freedom from War (The United States Program for General and Complete Disarmament in a Peaceful World)*, September 1961, p. 3.

26. Ibid., p. 19.

27. Nesta H. Webster, *Secret Societies and Subversive Movements*, 1924; Christian Book Club of America, pp. 218-219.

28. Rev. Clarence Kelly, *Conspiracy Against God and Man*, Western Islands, Boston, 1974, p.179.

29. Note 27, p. 218.

30. Note 28, pp. 178-179.

31. Texe Marrs, *Dark Secrets of the New Age*, Crossway Books, Westchester, IL, 1987, p. 198.

32. Note 1, pp. 309-310.

33. Ibid., p. 191.

34. George Orwell, *1984*, Signet, New York, 1949; 1950, pp. 61-62.

35. "CFR Members in the Media," *The New American*, 16 September 1996, pp. 18-19.

36. Note 1, pp. 190-191.

37. Note 34, p. 60.

38. Ibid., p. 61.

39. Ibid., p. 216.

40. Note 1, pp. 190-191.

41. Robert Conquest and Jon Manchip White, *What To Do When The Russians Come*, Stein and Day, New York, 1984, pp. 79-143.

42. Note 34, pp. 19-20.

43. Ibid., p. 54.

44. Ibid., p. 217.

45. Ibid., p. 24.

46. A. Ralph Epperson, *The Unseen Hand*, Publius Press, Tucson, 1985, pp. 252-253.

47. Gary Benoit, "Creating Global Crises," *The New American*, 16 September 1996, p. 50.

48. "Insider Report," *The New American*, 14 October 1996, p. 13.

49. Note 25.

50. Note 14, p. 35.

51. Texe Marrs, *Circle of Intrigue*, Living Truth Publishers, Austin, 1995, pp. 77-92.

52. Note 34, p. 171.

53. Note 1, p. 360.

54. Ibid., p. 191.

55. Note 14, p. 35.

56. Ibid.

57. Note 34, p. 220.

Index

N

S

T

U

About the Author

Edward E. Noble, a Vietnam-era veteran, is a former public school teacher with three graduate degrees. his chief interests are philosophy, literature, and art. He is also an inventor (currently holding two U.S. patents) and is listed in *Who's Who of American Inventors*, 1992-1993.